DEDICATION

This book is dedicated to my eternal *Isis-Magdalene Loretta Lucynda Hoffman*. My Love for you is unbounded. You have stood beside me from the beginning of Time itself. After countless lifetimes entwined beside each other as lovers, siblings, best friends and trusted companions, we continue to grow, evolve, share and love together. And this is my highest honor in this dimension of reality – to have the privilege of loving you and our beautiful children. Thank you for caring for us and keeping the home fires burning while I am out on the open road for weeks on end. You are allowing me to thread these beautiful filaments of light through so many open hearts across the earth.

You are my greatest support beyond words. I literally could not do this without you *Beautiful*, nor would I ever want to. You have never once voiced a single doubt as to whether I could realize this cosmic dream that burns in my heart 24 hours a day. You just knew. You always have.

This book is for you.

SPECIAL THANKS

For my Eternal family – Lucynda, Michael and Shemaya. I would be truly insane without each and every one of you. (*Maybe I already am?*) Not once have the three of you ever projected anything upon me for living my Life's Mission and spending so much time on the road away from our home. Not once. We are all in this together. I Love you all.

To Michael Ormond – my best friend of 33 years. You have never once worn a single mask in my presence, and for this I thank you. You were right beside me when I woke up from this intoxicating dream! I love you brother. To my amazing father Jack, who taught me how to love this world regardless of its ever changing appearances. To my "other mother" Cynthia Rose – your support is always there for us and thank you for birthing and raising the love of my life in this incarnation around the sun! My sister Denise and brother in law Michael O'Boyle. My Aunt Alma Obinger. Bob Sima and Shannon Plummer, you are my greatest sounding boards of love and light. I am honored to walk this path with you!

To Shelley Bibeau – a true friend and an amazing editor who "gets" what is flowing through me. Knowing that you can edit my Syriac is a definite plus! My spirit brother Steve Vai. Your never ending support continues to humble me. You are always there when I need you and to know that you truly love the work that is birthing through me brings a smile to my face. Dr Michael and Jeanie Ryce – thank you for continually reminding me that this dream is all between my ears and that I can always forgive and remove the root of my suffering from within my own heart. Corky Larsen and Barb Clugh – my Ohio family [CODED: ܗܝ ܡܢܚܪ ܗܘܪܛ ܢܐ ܦܟܡ ܟܝ]. Markus Bishop – my brother from another mother. Your unwavering support inspires me to continue my evolution, knowing that I will always have what I need when I need it. Joshua and Lauren Warren – our cohorts in conscious crime! Liz Cox – our Spirit Sister. Jeremy and Carmen Colson – your love and support for Jett can change this world! Thank you for passing the light on to the next generation! Shimshai – my high vibe brother! I am deeply honored to have your cosmic words on these pages! Self-Realization Fellowship in Los Angeles, CA. Michael Lightweaver – my dear Spirit Brother and steward of our home away from home Mountain Light Sanctuary. Tim Freke – for your lucidity and Gnosis. Gabriel Cavasos, Charles Gilchrist. Drs. John and Barbara Waterhouse – you both guided me toward further awakening my creative power. Hal Zina Bennett – thank you for your encouragement, guidance and inspiration! David Miller – my first best friend with whom I spent countless hours waaaaay back in the 1970's! Brian and Katy, Nana Hendricks, Mary Lou Houllis, Wendy Owens, Beecham Parker, Danielle Leigh, Charlotte McGinnis, Steve Kaczmarek, Tom Nehrer, Harold Ballen, Jim Ormond, Nic Paton and Voxi Choir, Everyone at Joyful Gathering Spiritual Center and Unity Fellowship Church – my spiritual homes away from home. Ceil and Dai, Padre Paul Funfsinn and everyone at Celebrating Life Ministries. Brian and Pam Crissey, David Byrley, Albert and Carol LaChance, Paulette Millichap, Rev Margaret Hiller, Kim Hughes. Stephen Simon, Suzanna Otting and everyone at GaiamTV and The Spiritual Cinema Circle, Rev Jesse Herriott, Dr. Steven Hairfield, Carol Guy, Bill Walz, Nicholas "The Bard" Andrea, Rev Rob Wheeler, Dr. Tim Hayes, Roi Klark, Steve Caruso at www.aramaicnt.org. David, Tammi and Jordan Hoffman. Sheri Rosenthal at Journeys of the Spirit. Susan Shumsky. Everyone at West End Bakery, where most of this book was written amidst the chaos of a busy West Asheville morning.

To the conscious life energy grids of Asheville, North Carolina; Mount Shasta, California and Lake Okeechobee, Florida – the three primary locations where this book was written.

To all of the venues who have the courage and vision to support this work and offer your spiritual families a much more accurate, calibrated truth. I commend you for your integrity and authenticity in a time when it is much easier to just market a persona and feed that to an often easily-hooked mass of souls. To all of the individual souls across the earth (and beyond) who have embraced and supported this mission. *I Love You All Eternally……*

TABLE OF CONTENTS

"Sound or vibration is the most powerful force in the universe. Music is a divine art, to be used not only for pleasure but as a path to God-realization. Vibrations resulting from devotional singing lead to attunement with the Cosmic Vibration or *The Word.*

In the beginning was the Word,
and the word was with God,
and the Word was God.
John 1:1"

PARAMAHANSA YOGANANDA
From the book "*Cosmic Chants*"
[Self-Realization Fellowship – Los Angeles, CA]

FOREWORD

"*Everything is Music*." All things in Creation are vibrational energies pulsating at various frequencies. On the physical plane we see, taste, feel, smell and hear vibrations that have frequencies within our sensory abilities to perceive them. The electrons spinning around the nucleus of an atom, the quarks within the nuclei and the elements that make up the subatomic quantum levels are vibrating within a frequency spectrum that is contributing to the creation of elements that are beyond the limitations of our human senses.

Similarly, but on a much larger scale, the planets that spin around our sun create a vibrational voice as the solar systems move within a galaxy within the infinite galaxies that move within the whole of physical creation, all weaving a multi-pitch celestial orchestra beyond the comprehension of the human senses.

On much subtler planes, thoughts are also vibrating within their own frequency spectrum. The vibration of a particular thought form sets into motion the elements that manifest its corresponding matter. These frequencies vibrate at the causal level which consists of extremely fine matter, but matter none the less.

Within this vast and virtually infinite spectrum of vibrations that make up the physical and ethereal worlds, human senses can perceive only within a minute, infinitesimal range. Yet all frequencies are upheld and nested within all others. All frequencies are interconnected in a vast, cosmic overtone series, the primordial pitch of which was struck in what we sometimes refer to as *The Big Bang*. Perhaps this initial propulsion may be more appropriately described as *The Primordial Ping*. Every vibration continues to proliferate from that first ping. All is built from it and it contains all that comes before and after it.

On the physical plane, when a person resonates with a particular vibration, be it a thought, sound or other sense perception, they are perceiving a tiny overtone of the whole. Yet because all parts are contained within the whole, certain words and sounds can resonate in a person as deeply and profoundly as that person is "in tune" to receive them. There are virtually no limits to the high or low ends of the entire frequency spectrum.

If a person's level of awareness is resonating at a high frequency then the finer, more crystalline overtones of pure vibrations, such as inner joy, peace, presence and the like can raise the entire vibrational frequency of the human to an even higher, more refined harmony within creation. If one is resonating at a low frequency such as anger, greed, fear, etc., they can be lured downward by the intense gravity of those lower frequencies into a chaotic distortion.

There are two elements at play here: One is the vibrations that can be considered all "things" which include the physical and ethereal dimensions. The other is the empty, silent space that all vibrations dance within. This empty space is no-thing but in essence is every-thing as it permeates and puts into motion all vibrations making all things both everything and nothing. This is the paradox of reality that the human mind in incapable of comprehending but the conscious awareness is capable of perceiving when "in tune".

The causal element of the creation of vibrations is thought. But before thought, there is the empty *no-thing-ness.* It is the unconditioned, timeless, infinite, never born, always has been, beyond all vibration, primal intelligence – the eternally conscious, aware space. All vibrations that resonate from this eternal nothingness eventually return to it and at that moment there is yet another ping. Each time this happens, all resonations are within an expanded and more refined frequency spectrum.

All vibrations within all frequencies which lie at the core of all things seen and unseen create a divine melody that is the primal life that resonates at the core of all things. This essential Life can be heard by humans in the deep stillness of the unconditioned, awakened consciousness that resides at the still point of all human beings. This sound current then seductively draws our lucid awareness back to the source of the primordial ping of all Life itself. That awareness then becomes aware of being all things in a state of eternal awakening.

If we call this omnipresent "no-thing-ness" source of all vibrations "God," then all vibrating frequencies, which is the entire creation itself, may be considered God's Symphony. In essence, everything is music. It is God's music, and it is God. *And he sure knows how to rock!*

In light of this, I have always been deeply fascinated with the "words" of Jesus and always hoped that someone would come along that could give meaningful and accurate translations of the writings and reveal the deeper teachings. Dale's translations and deep spiritual insight shows how the message of Jesus resonates with the sublime message of many of the great prophets – Buddha, Mohamed, Great Eastern Saints, Tolle etc. Dale's delivery is very grounded and sober and I believe his work is vital in the evolution of the awakening awareness of Human consciousness. *Enjoy the show!*

STEVE VAI
Musician – Los Angeles, CA

INTRODUCTION

Modern western figures such as Joseph Rael, Jonathan Goldman, Steven Halpern and Ted Andrews have brought vocal toning, or *intonation*, to the forefront of the early 21st century spiritual movement. Toning has had a steady rise since the late 1960's popularity of mantra singing and toning in North America along with Laurel Elizabeth Keyes trailblazing 1973 book "*Toning: The Healing Power of the Voice*" in 1973. Beyond its recent worldwide reemergence as "the next big thing", toning has been a central healing force of the spirit likely since the dawn of verbal human communication itself.

From Egyptian toning in the great pyramid, Inuit and Tibetan throat singing, Mongolian overtone singing, to the first nations of what is now the United States and to the Aborigines of central Australia, vocal toning has remained alive and well in indigenous cultures across the earth. The continuously growing popularity of Sanskrit *kirtan* and chanting in the west continues to expand our awareness of the power of consciously toned vocal processes in the healing and transmutation of our spiritual and physical health.

The phrase "sound health" has begun to take on an entirely new meaning as we reawaken into the power of sacred vibration and cosmic laws that we are now coming into a much richer realization of. After millennia of being relegated to the sidelines of popular culture and practiced mostly by esoteric mystics, toning is steadily becoming a nurturing, healing salve in these times of incessant environmental pollution and mass media overload for common everyday people.

In setting out to write this book, my central intention was on keeping this introductory volume as user friendly as possible. I am continually being told by new toners how discouraged they are picking up a book on toning and sound healing only to be bombarded by excessively complex analogies and simply too many details without ever actually "getting to the point". I am committed to making *Echoes of an Ancient Dream* accessible enough to be readable for newbies as well as deeply rewarding for even the most ardently committed spiritual seekers and practitioners.

My focus in this first book will be in offering not only my own personal experience and story with the power of vocal toning, but specifically with a focus on my daily practice of toning the ancient Aramaic words of *Yeshua*, aka. *Jesus of Nazareth.* Incidentally, the Aramaic word *natzariyt* means "inititate". I will focus in future books and teaching programs on the much more primal processes of utilizing the power of toning as an expression of primordial vibration as well as offering many more specific words, sounds and phrases for experimentation.

Laurel Elizabeth Keyes often used the succinct analogy of likening vocal toning to the response of moving a magnet around beneath iron filings assembled on a glass slide or the influence of sound on salt crystals scattered upon a drum head. Not only do these filings and salt crystals shift around, but they in fact create fractal patterns in resonance with the forces influencing their movement. The natural energetic vibrations of the intention and sound directly affect what we refer to as physical matter.

In his book "*USE THE FORCE: A Jedi's Guide to the Law of Attraction*," my friend Joshua P. Warren reminds us that the three most powerful words that we can use in the English language to instantaneously "*wipe out the dark energy that plagues our mind*" are "*I love you.*" I could not agree more. In fact, a unique quality of many ancient and indigenous languages is that the root sounds were, and are, believed to be specific vibrational expressions of the very energetic frequencies that they "mean" when spoken.

In other words, these specific sounds are believed to bring one into awareness of the direct experience that the sound is defined as. As an example, the primary Aramaic word for "love" or "friend" is *rakhma.* The belief is that consciously speaking or toning rakhma activates the vibration of love itself. This profound spiritual practice also has deep roots in ancient *Gnosticism.* The Greek word *gnosis,* pronounced "no-sis" meant "knowledge". However, the modern understanding of the word knowledge can no longer hold the ancient meaning of gnosis. A better modern English definition of the ancient word gnosis would be "direct experience." Gnosis is not about a mental understanding, it is about a much deeper, wholly experiential *realization.*

The pioneering work of Dr. Marasru Emoto in his groundbreaking book "*The Hidden Messages in Water*" have re-affirmed the power of intentional force upon our manifest "reality". Dr. Emoto shared how human intention and consciousness has a direct effect on the molecular structure of water. Of course, Dr. Emoto's work is often dismissed as nothing more than "pseudo-science" because much of his research fell outside of the much more widely accepted and clearly defined limitations of what science is able to perceive or comprehend. In other words, if it is outside of our senses or monitoring equipment's abilities to perceive it, then it must not be "real".

I am quite sure that this will be more emphatically projected upon toning as it continues to become much more widespread and gain in popularity. It may have seemed nearly crazy 30 years ago to envision practices like meditation, yoga and reiki in modern hospitals, yet more and more medical centers are beginning to offer these practices as a holistic compliment to allopathic medicine. I believe that within twenty years, toning will be offered in many hospitals as well. I may sound crazy now, but mark my words, it is on the way.

All this being said, *Echoes of an Ancient Dream* is not simply a book about Aramaic toning or looking deeper into the "words" of Jesus. Toning is about tuning into and expressing the vibrational essence or "voice" of Life Itself. This is a book about allowing ourselves to feel and embrace the much more intangible and experiential feminine qualities of life and spirituality. A cognitive intellectual understanding of what mysticism is will never get you into the direct experience itself. And this is why I am so enthusiastic about vocal toning in my life's work.

I can talk out of both sides of my mouth for hours on end about what an Aramaic word "means" without ever actually realizing the tone of its experiential voice in my heart. The process of consciously intoning a word or sound is the fastest, most efficient process that I have ever encountered for shifting the state of one's mind back into the balance of Presence. Mediation, prayer, yoga, breath work and the like all have their essential place in the healer's toolkit for awakening. Yet, it is vocal toning that allows us to almost immediately feel this dramatic calibration back into the present moment in a matter of three or four seconds. The experience is virtually instantaneous, even for a newcomer.

I am excited to share several of my most profound experiences with you as I discovered (re-discovered?) the immense power of vocal toning and the rich insights and wisdom embedded within the Aramaic Yeshua teachings in my life. My conscious, often rocky relationship with the Holy Bible reaches all the way back to when I was seven years old. It is of central importance to me that we come to embrace the poignant truth that the musings of a seven-year-old child are just as important as those of an "expert" in their seventh decade of life. We must embrace our innocence and our authentic light because we are the ones that we have been waiting for!

ܕܬܚܒܘܢ ܚܕ ܠܚܕ ܐܝܟܢܐ ܕܐܢܐ ܐܚܒܬܟܘܢ

d'tkhboun khd l'khd aykanah d'ena akhb'tkoun
Love one another as I have loved you,

DALE ALLEN HOFFMAN
Asheville, NC

Section One

ESSENCE: *My Journey Back to the Beginning*

"Om Shabbat Shalom, Holy Way of the Most High
Om Shabbat Shalom, I sense Your Presence

I Am the light within your soul
In the essence of truth and right, love makes the circle whole
And here we stand in line, waiting for some sacred sign
But to find the balance is the purpose of this time
To restore the balance of the Universal Mind

And in the presence of my Lord of light and love
Everything I see aspiring to be free
And when I call to Thee and come on bended knee
Surrender to the all-pervading light and love
Reflections of the One surrounding me with love

I sense Your Presence

Within and without, above and below
East, west, north and south
I sense Your Presence
Without and within, below and above
East, west, north and south

I sense Your Presence.

SHIMSHAI
"I Sense Your Presence"
[From the album *Toward the One*]

CHAPTER 1

OPENING THE GOD BOX

It was just after 3am on a Saturday morning in June 1995. After tossing and turning in bed for over an hour, I got up and wandered out into the quiet living room of the main house called *Eternity* which was set up for the support team at Heartland Aramaic Mission, Dr. Michael Ryce's teaching center in the Ozark Mountains of Missouri. I had signed on for the summer as a member of Heartland's support team who would arrive several weeks earlier than the general summer intensive attendees to prepare the grounds and buildings for the season. In return for our weeks of hard work, we would benefit from the direct, focused experience of learning to practice the ancient Aramaic process of forgiveness as exemplified in the teachings of *Yeshua*, aka "Jesus". Each evening after dinner, we learned how to assist others with their own forgiveness processing.

I kneeled down beside a small end table and began digging through a cardboard box of cassette tapes that had been sitting in the corner of the room for several weeks now. As I searched through the box, I kept seeing two names which registered in my mind as George Llama and Enrico Caruso. In truth they were recordings by *Dr. George Lamsa* and *Dr. Rocco Errico.* Though I did not know it at the time, the late Dr. Lamsa was a man who had been largely credited half a century earlier with bringing the ancient near eastern Aramaic teachings of Jesus to "commoners" in the West, and in particular, to the English language. Dr. Errico was Lamsa's only personal Aramaic student. I also did not yet know that it was Dr. Errico who was Dr. Ryce's original inspiration with the Aramaic teachings almost 20 years earlier.

As I continued spinning cassettes around in the box, one title jumped out at me: "The Aramaic Prayer of Jesus" by Dr. Rocco Errico. I popped it into a boom box sitting on the end table and pushed play. *"Hello, this is Dr. Rocco Errico! And welcome to the Aramaic prayer of Jesus!"* I immediately connected with his voice. He continued by saying that he was going to recite the ancient Aramaic Prayer of Jesus.

And then I heard it.

"Ahhhhhhhwoon dwashmaya! Nitqadash shmakh! Tey tey malkootak!"

My head started to spin and I lost all sense of where I was and what was happening as Dr. Errico continued with the prayer. I had a familiar vision that I had been having since I was a child, of a spiral galaxy full of glistening stars swirling above my head. And I knew it immediately – *this is it.* This is exactly why I am here on earth. To tell everyone about *THIS.*

I spent the next hour trying to speak the first few lines of the Aramaic Lord's Prayer. But I kept coming back to that first word.

"Ahhhhhhwoooooon."

Something about that sound felt so achingly intimate and familiar to me, though I had never heard it before in my life. *Or had I?* It was almost as if I knew exactly what each and every vibration within the prayer meant, though in truth I had no earthly idea about *any* of it. It just resonated so deeply within my soul. I stopped the cassette and sat on the floor, my mind still reeling, continuing to almost sing that sound three times.

"Ahhhhhhwoooooon."

"Ahhhhhhwoooooon."

"Ahhhhhhwoooooon."

I sat in in silence as the trailing after-effect of the tones continued echoing throughout my body.

"Ahhhhhhwoooooon."

I was acutely aware of the rise and fall of my breath. It was as if I was inhaling the entire universe into my lungs and exhaling spiral clusters of sparkling stars out of my mouth into the room around me. I realized that I was observing my body from above and behind my right shoulder, as if my awareness had dislocated itself outside of my brain and found a hovering space to observe "me."

I remembered what Carlos Castaneda spoke of in his book *The Power of Silence*. His teacher, Yaqui master *Don Juan Matus*, had helped Carlos get in touch with what he called the "assemblage point." The assemblage point is the epicenter of the human energy field. By manipulating Castaneda's assemblage point, Don Juan could suddenly trigger Carlos' consciousness to shift into different dimensions of what we call "reality."

I thought "*Is that what this is? Or is this something else?*" While I'd had several transcendent experiences over the years through meditation, this was the first time that I had ever felt this. I sat in silence on the floor and gazed at the foliage of a large oak tree just outside the open window in front of me, dimly lit by the lamp in the corner of the room. The cool night air was flowing through the screen and tickling the hairs on my forearm as it whirled across my skin. I felt wide open and at absolute peace, though also buzzing with inner activity.

After several minutes of unmoving stillness, I mindfully stood up and reached for a canoe paddle that was leaning against the door frame beside me. As I walked outside onto a small patch of damp grass, I envisioned my feet having roots descending thousands of miles into the center of the molten core of the earth. I felt as if I was drawing the earth's sacred energy up through the soles of my feet, which were now burning.

I stood outside in the clear, moonless night and stared at the tree that I had been peering through the open window at just a few moments earlier. The tree was active in a way that I had not sensed since I was a child. Tiny filaments and swirling patterns of geometric figures were dancing inside and around the leaves while being fed by a natural flowing energetic river up its trunk from out of the depths of the earth. Amidst the darkness of the early morning, the natural world all around me was alive with gleaming halos and dancing spirals of light.

I turned toward my right and began walking down the dirt road toward Bull Shoals Lake as tiny stones crunched and popped beneath my bare feet. My awareness was riding on the waves of my breath as the echoing vibrations of those Aramaic tones continued reverberating within my body, now several minutes in my past. After some time, I reached the top of the final slope down toward the grassless, rocky shoreline of the lake.

I could feel the buzz of my earlier Aramaic sound experience beginning to wane a bit as I made my way down the hill to a canoe tied to a wooden stake along the shoreline. I realized that I had made my way down to the lake without a flashlight, guided only by my inner knowing and the softest hint of starlight peeking through the trees. I hadn't even thought about bringing a flashlight until now. I had just started walking.

I slid the paddle into the canoe, untied the nylon rope and slipped the canoe into the glassy mountain water. The rings riding on the surface of the water were very similar in their outward circles of motion to the light threads I observed on the tree in the yard up the hill. I gently paddled away from the shore and could see the subtle reflection of the stars in the night sky on the water all around me. I seemed to sense more than see the starlight mirroring its glowing breath on the face of the deep water.

As I made my way further out of our cove and into the greater expanse of the main lake, I found myself silently toning *"Ahhhhhhwoooooon"* almost subconsciously before pausing to bathe in the tone's centering afterglow. I continued gently paddling and toning for several minutes before sliding into a much quieter, less developed cove surrounded by sheer rock walls about a quarter mile away from my launching point.

I glided my canoe across the water to the center of the cove and stopped rowing, allowing the canoe's momentum to slowly recede before gently resting on the subtle ebb and flow of the lake's surface. I sat in absolute stillness for several long minutes until the ripples around the canoe finally quieted down and ceased into a sheet of liquid glass. I closed my eyes and remained motionless, hardly breathing, so as not to disturb the smooth surface of the lake around me.

As I opened my eyes some time later, I could not miss the intensifying vibration of a tone that seemed to be expanding from within the center of my chest, though I was still and not making a sound. I paid curious attention as it opened itself within my heart. I again felt that my awareness was wide open as I observed the growing sound:

"Ahhhhhhwoooooon." Or was it *"Aum?"*

To this day, I am not sure which of those two tones that I was feeling that morning, though I have come to realize that they may in fact be two perceptions of one sacred cosmic tone that is, in the words of Paramahansa Yogananda perceived as a *"superconscious chant"* more than heard as an actual word.

I gently began to tone that Aramaic word again,

"Ahhhhhhwoooooon."

I opened my eyes and saw rings on the surface of the water emanating from the canoe and expanding outward across the water in the starlight. The rings were speckled with the reflected stars now appearing to dance and surf across the tiny spirals expanding outward from the canoe.

"Ahhhhhhhhhhh – woooooooon."

"Ahhhhhhhhhhhhhhhh – wooooooooooooooon."

The rings began to return from the shoreline and fuse with those pushing their way out from the canoe. Their relationship began forming patterns much like those I saw in the large oak tree earlier in a dazzling universal dance of shimmering light. As I continued toning, I was aware of the relationship of the sound as it was leaving my mouth, as it journeyed through the air, and its tinny reflection from the water as it returned to me. I continued to tone and to be aware.

"Ahhhhhhhhhhhhhhhh – wooooooooooooooon."

The echoes of these profound vibrations were beginning to bounce back from the rock walls surrounding my cozy womb in the center of the cove and were now comingling with the other tones circling within and around me. All of these beautiful waves were coming together in a beautiful cosmic ballet of vibration, light and movement. Deep in the center of my heart, I knew I was home.

"They [adolescents] now seem to love luxury, they have bad manners and contempt for authority. They show disrespect for adults and spend their time hanging around places gossiping with one another. They are ready to contradict their parents, monopolize the conversation and company, eat gluttonously and tyrannize their teachers."

SOCRATES
circa 400 B.C.

CHAPTER 2

COMING HOME TO A PLACE I'D NEVER BEEN BEFORE

As the dancing water rings around me began to subside, I sat motionless in the canoe, allowing my thoughts to drift back to my everyday senses as the soft feminine glow of the sun began to peek over the hills in the distance. Over the next two decades I would have many more equally profound yet unique experiences that would often transport me back to that dark and starry morning on the lake. As the sun continued to rise over the lake, I thought of how dramatically my spiritual life had transformed over the previous two years.

In June 1993 I rolled into the back seat of a black Chevy Beretta for a thousand-mile road trip from my home in the rural farmlands of southern New Jersey down to the gulf coast of Florida. I was twenty-one and was moving down with a few friends of mine to share a 400 square foot one-bedroom apartment with at least six other early twenty-somethings' as well as an occasional runaway or underappreciated wanderer.

In Florida, I soon began attending an *A Course in Miracles* study group in Indian Rocks Beach just two blocks from the Gulf of Mexico. After spending well over a year attending Marianne Williamson's ACIM monthly talks at New York's Town Hall as well as her study groups at the New York Open Center, I was elated to find a group near my new home.

Right from my first Course gathering in Indian Rocks Beach, I began to hear the name Dr. Michael Ryce quite often. After a few months I joined in with a weekly men's group that gathered in a home on the beach every Friday evening to practice Stillpoint Breathing. Stillpoint Breathing is a technique that had been re-developed by Dr. Ryce after his experiences with Leonard Orr's rebirthing movement of the 1970's and 80's. The roots of intentional breath work thread back thousands of years in cultures across the earth, including with luminaries such as *St. Theresa of Avila* and *Paramahansa Yogananda.* I have been a certified StillPoint Breathing Practitioner since 1995 and still find it to be the most thorough and effective breath work process I have ever encountered.

In the spring of 1995, a few people in the ACIM group were talking about Michael Ryce coming to Clearwater Florida in a few weeks to present a week's worth of workshops based on the Aramaic teachings of Jesus. My questions and responses were pretty comical.

"Arabic?"

"No, Aramaic."

"Aromatic?"

"Yeah, that means that Jesus smelled really good!"

"Huh?"

"Aramaic?" I said. *"What's that?"*

"Aramaic is the language that Jesus spoke"

"He didn't speak English?"

Everyone began laughing.

"English didn't even exist then!"

I never before even thought about what language Jesus would have spoken – never crossed my mind – not once. Not needing to hear anything more about this Dr. Ryce guy, I knew I had to be there.

The evening was one of those experiences that is a milestone in my life, the significance of which cannot be measured. I sat near the back of the room in the last row of seats just in case I felt the need to make an undetected escape. I watched and listened to Dr. Ryce and his workshop *'Why is This Happening to Me....AGAIN?!'*. I literally sat on my hands to keep myself from jumping up onto my chair and yelling *"Yes!"* at the top of my lungs. I was stunned, at times nearly breathless, hearing him speak for the first time.

This guy was validating my deepest thoughts and feelings about the biblical teachings of Jesus that I'd had in my gut since I was a child. He was revealing a much deeper truth about how the original Aramaic teachings were much more accurate than what I had been programmed to believe in all of my years of being raised on a steady diet of church, Sunday school, vacation Bible school and family "Bible thrashings."

Even at the age of seven, I instinctively knew that all of the not so lovely experiences that go along with indoctrination and manmade ideological religious warfare was nothing more than someone trying to push their beliefs about Jesus onto me so as to keep from concealing the realization that they in truth had absolutely no idea how to actually LIVE what Jesus taught. I understood that even though you may be able to quote the definition of a word, that does not in any way require that you actually understand what the word really *means*. Children are born with this authentic clarity. Regardless of whether they ever express it to their elders or not, it is there.

I had never before heard anyone put into words the things I had been *feeling* about the teachings of Jesus since I was five or six years old. As a child, I would often look around the room and realize that I was usually the only one present who did not have exactly the same, homogenous opinion about the meanings of the teachings of Jesus as everyone else seemed to spend so much energy clutching on to. Even at such a young age, I did not want to hold on – I wanted to let go. And I wanted everyone else around me to let go too.

The lucidity of Dr. Ryce's words continued to peel me open as my body began to shake and shudder. I was crying, I was laughing, my nose was running, it was a complete overload of my system and I was loving it! As I approached him during the mid-workshop break, I was still shaking, red faced and drenched with sweat. He took a good look at me and said *"It looks like I could peel you off the ceiling young man! What's happening?"*

I responded *"I don't even know what's going on right now but whatever it is that you have, I want it. ALL of it."*

Three months later, there I was at Heartland digging through that box of audio cassettes, completely unaware of how profoundly the depth and arc of my life would be transformed in less than 20 minutes. This nearly mythic adventure has taken me to places, geographically and spiritually, that I could never have imagined when I was feeling like the "odd man out" in my very ordinary Methodist church upbringing.

I remember that Sunday school class at the age of seven as I looked at my teacher and around the room toward all of the other kids when something I had been feeling in my gut for quite some time finally popped into my field of vision. Every single one of them seemed to have exactly the same opinion about the Bible verses from the teachings of Jesus that we had been reviewing for the past several weeks. I, however, did not. I never seemed to see or hear Jesus's teachings the same way everyone else did. Ever.

I went for seven more years before I realized that this may actually be a *good* thing. I had already begun reading the entire King James Bible cover to cover when I was seven, often penciling in notes and "clarifications" above the text as well as in depth commentary around the margins. I had also memorized all of the book titles of the Old and New Testaments, forward and backward and could recite them on command, just like a trained memory monkey.

It was at the age of seven in 1979 that I first laid five of my grandmother Irene's different bible's out on her living room floor and opened them up to the beatitudes from the Gospel of Matthew. I was stunned to learn that the beatitudes as they were written in each of those five bibles were so obviously different in their meanings and content that I actually began to feel nauseous and dizzy. I had no idea at the time what this ick in the pit of my stomach meant, but I knew it was not necessarily a good thing. *Or maybe it was.*

I recently found my childhood bible that had been given to my mother by her mother – my grandmother Irene – for Christmas in 1956. I suspect that my grandmother was probably hoping that the holiness of the pages would somehow rub off on my mom to calm her down a bit and get her off of that Elvis and rock and roll kick she was on at the time. When I was seven years old I had asked my mother if I could have it, knowing that she did not have much use for it. When I came upon the bible a few years ago while rummaging through a box, I immediately opened it and looked around inside. Right there in the front of the book were five of my favorite beatitudes from the Gospel of Matthew, scrawled in pencil by my seven-year-old hand:

"Blessed are they which are persecuted for righteousness' sake,
for theirs is the kingdom of heaven"
Matthew 5:10 KJV (King James Version)

"Blessed are ye, when men shall revile you, and persecute you, and say all manner of evil against you falsely, for my sake."
Matthew 5:11 KJV

"Rejoice, and be exceeding glad: for great is your reward in heaven: for so persecuted they the prophets which were before you."
Matthew 5:12 KJV

Blessed are they which do hunger and thirst after righteousness: for they shall be filled."
Matthew 5:6 KJV

"Blessed are the Peacemakers (I had that word capitalized!): for they shall be called the children of God."
Matthew 5:9 KJV

I would read the bible for hours on any given day, very often deep in the woods where no one would laugh or bother me about it. I began noticing that when I allowed myself to be very still and ride on the waves of my breath that I was able to sense meanings threaded through the words attributed to Jesus that I couldn't even see when I was just in a normal everyday state of mind. These insights would usually just take on a greater awareness of the meaning of his words and teachings, though on a few occasions, it was a much more profound experience than anything that my young mind could fully comprehend at the time.

It was mid-summer of 1979 and I was in a vacation bible school class at our church in the small town of Clarksboro, New Jersey. Our class was deep in a discussion of the "*lay up for yourselves treasures in heaven*" verses in Matthew Chapter 6. Everyone else was talking about heaven as some place that we go to only after we die. They spoke of "laying up treasures in heaven" as if they were "brownie points", as if a man named God was somehow going to keep tabs on us and reward us for being good little soldiers when we die. *What????* It made no sense at all to me. It still doesn't.

In his modern classic book "*Meeting Jesus Again for the First Time,*" Marcus Borg wrote about the first *theological conundrum* that he experienced as a child. He recalled being puzzled by the incongruence of being told that God was somehow both "*everywhere present*" and yet also "*up in heaven*" simultaneously. He wrote "*without realizing it, I was wrestling with the relationship between the omnipresence and the transcendence of God.*" Looking back on my own childhood from the perspective of who I am today, I felt much the same myself.

Episcopalian priest Cynthia Bourgeault says that Jesus's parables are, much like a *Zen koan,* meant to "*fry our sockets,*" to force our rational, thinking mind to implode upon itself and finally *let go.* The immense depth of these eternal jewels of wisdom must be experientially *realized* rather than simply mentally understood, as if that mental understanding were often even possible. In their essential, must – read book "*Jesus and the Lost Goddess*", Tim Freke and Peter Gandy reveal that if we become overly engrossed with the words on the page, as literalists do, rather than remaining open to their much deeper underlying *essence*, then we unknowingly "*mistake the message for the meaning and end up eating the menu, not the meal.*"

Now in my forties, I can very clearly see that some spark within my young mind was attempting to remain open rather than locked down in the conceptual theology that was being force fed to me on an almost daily basis. I was supposed to sit down, keep quiet and "*eat the meal being served.*" Thankfully though, I did sit still, keep quiet and eat what was being served for some time, I was able to know in my heart that something much greater lay beyond the horizon. These experiences strengthened my resolve to always question the veracity of what I was told, and to trust my own ability to investigate further, outside of the theological fences that the church advised us to never venture beyond, on pain of death.

At the time, though, I was not thinking that I was right and they were wrong, but rather the exact opposite. I thought that something was wrong with *me*, that I just didn't "get it" – whatever "it" was. I was as usual not feeling the same way everyone else was about these words and found myself having a similar feeling throughout my body that I did when I would sit silently for hours in the woods, sailing on my breath. My face and neck began to burn as I looked around the room and then back down onto the pages of my bible.

Right there on the page, somehow behind and between the red words of Jesus, were characters and letters that I did not recognize, also in red. They did not look like English letters and I was not even really sure that I was seeing something "real" at all. I squeezed my eyes shut and rubbed them with my knuckles before opening them again and looking down at the page. The characters that had been there had been replaced by different characters, also not English. I had never seen anything like this before.

I stared down at the letters as a wave of some kind of feeling of what I would today call melancholy swept over me. I began to "feel" the meanings of the words in front of me, not necessarily the English words or the foreign characters, but somehow I felt ALL of it at once. I laid the bible flat in my open left hand, brought my right hand down toward the page and laid my fingertips against the characters. I wasn't sure that I was feeling anything out of the ordinary, so I pulled my hand back and looked up. The room was empty.

I could hear the voices of my teacher and the other students out in the hallway of the church, their voices like tiny shrill echoes bouncing off of the tile floor. My teacher poked her head back in the doorway and said very tersely:

"Are you coming?"

I stood up, my body still buzzing and my face and neck still burning like fire.

"What did you do?" she asked, probably in response to the look of shock on my face, like a kid caught red handed with his hand in a cookie jar.

I did not say a word as I walked out into the hallway, leaving her to survey the room for proof of my sins. We made our way down the red brick steps and out to the small playground behind the church. I had a very peculiar feeling that still lingered inside of me. It was not necessarily a good or bad feeling, just something that felt "not normal" to me. I remember feeling that it was not unlike the slight buzz I would feel after taking my Benadryl before my excursions outdoors, just in case I encountered a venomous sting, which happened quite often. The difference was that unlike my allergy medication, this feeling somehow hyper-sensitized how I felt, as if opening me up from within, rather than numbing me and making me feel spacey. Rather than *feeling* spacey, I somehow felt as if I was *space itself*. My eyes still tear up at the thought of it.

As I stood alone in the middle of a grassy field beside the screaming kids at the playground, I was very aware that my teacher was still staring at me, likely wondering what I was guilty of. It was one of the last days of vacation bible school and she was probably wondering if I was going to create any problems for her before it concluded later that week. She kept watching me and yet, for some reason, I could not have cared any less about her piercing glare.

A warm breeze was whistling through the trees that framed the back area of the church. I continued to gaze at the playing children and the waving trees around me, hearing a very faint, high pitched whining or wheezing sound in the breeze that I had never noticed before. It was a lot like those times when my ears would build up pressure during a lingering cold. I would hold my nose and try to "pop" my ears. Not a good thing, I know, but when you're a kid, you just do what comes naturally.

After my ears would pop, I could sense a sheen or what I would today call *presence*, as if I had been listening to music through speakers that had been covered with a blanket. Now, with the blanket removed, I could sense a brilliance all around me that I somehow knew had always been there, yet outside of my normal realm of awareness. I walked over to an old red brick fireplace in the corner of the church yard and just sat there, watching the other children playing and screaming in the afternoon sun. The feeling began to subside over the next half hour as I began to come back to my usual senses, though somehow, that presence had remained there, quietly resting, waiting for its next opportunity to re-emerge.

Growing up the young grandson of a pillar of our local Methodist church, which Irene most definitely was, I was expected to attend church like clockwork, though by that time my mom was old enough to somehow wiggle out of it. I didn't mind so much though. My maternal grandmother Irene would even drive around all over town after dropping my brother, sister and I off at the church. She would make as many trips back out as needed to pick up children and teens from around the area who wanted to attend church but otherwise wouldn't have due to the work schedule, or just a flat out disinterest, from their parents.

My brother and sister and I eventually began attending two churches on Sunday mornings. Though I don't remember where the idea came from, we would attend the early Sunday morning church services and Sunday school classes at our Evangelical United Methodist Church before walking to the Episcopalian church a block away. I was enamored with the Episcopal Church. I now call it *"Catholic–lite"*. The church's abundance of dark woods, gleaming candles, streams of light through the many stained glass windows and its intentional pageantry was enrapturing for a kid my age. Even there in the Episcopal Church though, I still felt like a black sheep – *different.* Like I just didn't get it. Yet somehow, I felt totally at home within the *energy* of the place.

Decades later, when I was poring over ancient texts, I did in fact recognize those letters that I was seeing in the bibles as a child. The first ones were Greek. I recognized the second letters as the *Ashurit* characters of the Hebrew and, for a time, Aramaic alphabets. Even today, as I spend hours staring at huge digital enlargements of ancient texts, I remember those first experiences as a child, when I began to "read between the lines."

It was also only after my steady approach into mid-life that I recognized that the gut and heart-level musings of a seven-year-old child can quite often be much more truthful and accurate than those of many heavily-conditioned, well-educated biblical experts with over 7 decades of study behind them. I must always keep my heart and mind open. No matter how much I think I know beyond any shadow of a doubt, I must forever be the humble student with more to learn. I always keep this understanding central in my awareness.

My young heart knew then what I often discover myself trying to learn now many decades later. I knew in my heart even then that the "heaven" Jesus was referring to was not simply a place that we go to after we drop our human coil. I somehow sensed, though not yet completely, that heaven existed right here and right now, in this present moment – in the Presence that I felt, saw and somehow even *heard* through that family bible so long ago.

The disciples said to Jesus, *"Tell us how our end will come."*

Jesus said, "*Have you discovered, then, the beginning,*
that you look for the end?
For where the beginning is, there will the end be.
Blessed is the one who takes his place in the beginning;
He will know the end and will not taste death.
Blessed is the one who came into being before he came into being."

THE COPTIC GOSPEL OF THOMAS *"THE TWIN"*

CHAPTER 3

FALLING BACK INTO THE ONE

The autumn morning that my mother died in October 2007 will be forever etched in my heart as the moment that I finally "got" the profound transformational magnitude of the simple act of toning even the most basic sounds, regardless of what they may "mean" in any particular language. I came into the intimate realization that it is not about the conceptual definition of what the sounds *mean*, but rather that the richness of the experience is embedded within our openness to get within the words and *feel the vibrations themselves.*

Just three days before that October morning with my mother in Southern New Jersey, I was at the Center for Spiritual Living in Asheville, North Carolina. It was about 20 minutes into their 11am Sunday celebration service and I was seated in the front row, about to walk up onto the stage to offer a toning meditation of the ancient Aramaic beatitudes of Yeshua from the *Gospel of Mattai* (Matthew). I would be offering these ancient sounds as a "taste" of what everyone may expect if they were to attend my *Five Aramaic Layers of Conscious Creation* gathering later that afternoon.

In the moment, I was hyper-aware of the reality that my mother was lying on her death bed hundreds of miles away. But I knew that I had to be right here, right now, and to do what I was about to do, before I could go to her in her final hours. My sister Denise had told me that she was sure that mom was holding on before she let go, waiting to see me one last time. I could feel my mother's heart echoing deep within my own heart and I could feel her yearning voice calling me back home as soon as my work here was complete.

I sat in my seat, barely in this dimension of reality, repeatedly mouthing the Aramaic words *"tey tey malkoota"*, *"tey tey malkoota"*, *"tey tey malkoota"* – "*thy kingdom come*" – quietly within myself, over and over and over. As I sat there, I began to experience a sensation that was quite new to me, yet somehow felt very familiar on a deeply intimate level. It was a throbbing, humming tone that I was *feeling* more than hearing. This enormous astronomical pumping or pulsation was continually growing inside of me with such a rapid intensity that I felt I may be about to lose consciousness altogether and drop to the ground.

I have come to call this experience the "*Cosmic Freight Train.*" This inter-dimensional adventure ride has happened to me several times since then, most notably during the opening waves of my first *Santo Daime ayahuasca* shamanic medicine journey two years later, as well as during the birth of my youngest daughter *Shemaya* and when I offer intensive psychic healing sessions with water and sacred oils.

In less than 20 seconds, this expanding "woofing" had become so intense and strong that I could hardly hear the words of Rev. Barbara Waterhouse on stage, who I was pretty sure was announcing what I was about to step up and do. And then I heard *"Dale Hoffman!"* I stood up, my entire body pulsating and shaking. By this point, my mind was completely empty and blank. I knew I was supposed to be walking up there to Barbara but I had absolutely no idea whatsoever why I was doing it.

About halfway to the steps leading up to the stage, I felt a strong buzzing pressure on my forehead, as if someone was pressing their thumb outward from inside of my head while wearing one of those cheap little magic trick buzzers I use to play with as a child. My entire head was engulfed on all sides by a loud hissing *"sssssssssssss"* tone for several seconds as my eyesight was filled with a burst of golden sparkles followed by an enormous *POP!* And then absolute silence – *nothing.*

For a moment, I felt like I was lying flat on the carpet before realizing that I was still walking forward and was about to ascend the three steps onto the stage. I did not have the faintest idea how I was walking and I did not feel that I was involved in that process in any way.

That is when I heard "it," very clearly spoken from deep within me and yet somehow not spoken at all:

"It is okay to let go, because you can only fall back into me."

I nearly collapsed in response to the immense wave of energy that surged through me as these words arose. Somehow, I found myself up on the stage, wrapped in Barbara's embrace before she placed a microphone into my hand and stepped away. As I moved forward, I was shaking so much that I was sure that every single person in the room must have been wondering what my problem was. The microphone was shaking so intensely in my hand that I popped it back into its clip and held on to that mic stand for dear life, my entire body still trembling and quaking. I somehow rattled off a short bit of an introduction before eventually sliding into my speaking of the Aramaic beatitudes. I closed my eyes and began.

"Toubveyhoun l'maskena b'rookh d'dilhoun hey malkoota d'shmaya"

"Toubveyhoun l'abviley d'hinnoun netbeyoun"

"Toubveyhoun l'makikey d'hinoun nertoun l'ahreah"

"Toubveyhoun leyleyn d'kaphneen wahtseyn l'kianouta d'hinoun nesboun"

"Toubveyhoun l'mrakhmaney d'leyhoun newheoun rakhma"

And then I went completely blank. Nothing. I had no idea where I was or what was happening. My body was shaking so uncontrollably that I felt like I was sitting atop a freight car on a wobbly rail line, almost unable to maintain my grip and hold on with little more than the very tips of my fingers.

I felt as if hours were passing before my eyes. I had no concept of linear time in any way that I had ever experienced it before. I very slowly opened my eyes and was somehow surprised to find myself on a stage in front of several hundred people, all seated with their eyes closed. But something was different. Everyone appeared to be threaded together and connected by thousands of tiny filaments of shimmering light. It was like the chasing white Christmas light strings that I saw during the holiday season, though these strings were much subtler and somehow almost invisible in the physical sense.

I closed my eyes again and paid attention to my breath. I had an echoing thought that I was reciting the beatitudes, though I had no idea what the next one was. None. Blotto. So I waited. And I waited some more. I slowly opened my eyes again, this time only squinting. The entire room was filled with one, intensely brilliant yet somehow warmly nurturing pool of light. The threads were now gone and all that I saw was light, though somehow it was more sensed than seen. It was as if I were perceiving an immense, eternal depth of being that was so pure that it emanated an Eternal light from within me. I saw it, and I *was* it.

Knowing that no one in the audience was counting how many beatitudes I had recited, and knowing that there was a pretty slim chance that anyone there spoke Aramaic, I just skipped over the sixth beatitude and just started reciting the seventh:

"Toubveyhoun l'abvdaye shlama d'whnaoie d'Alaha nitqaroun"

The sixth Aramaic beatitude had simply vanished. Gone without a trace. It was not until several months later when my friend Shanna asked me "*Dale, which beatitude was it that you blanked out on?*" that it hit me. Every single hair on my body seemed to stand on end in response to her question:

"Toubveyhoun leyleyn dadcean b'liboun d'hinoiun nekhzoun l'Alaha"
"Blessed are the pure in heart, for they shall see God"

Wow. That second Sunday of October 2007 began one of the most intense, yet deeply transformative growth periods of my entire life. After my workshop that afternoon, I made the announcement to the hundred or so audience members that "*Anyone wanting to stay for my sacred water healing ceremony can take a quick break and meet me back here in ten minutes. To everyone who is leaving, thank you so much for the honor of sharing this time with you!*" I then made my way straight to the men's room, expecting maybe 10 or 15 people to stay behind.

When I returned to the sanctuary to begin the water healing, I was not at all expecting what I saw. *Everyone was still there!* While I was out of the room, everyone had joined together to clear the chairs and stack them against the walls before one hundred people stood hand in hand in a circle in the center of the room, facing inward. I thought to myself "*What am I supposed to do NOW?*"

I did my best to stay in the moment and proceed. I had been getting intuitive hits for several weeks prior to the event that I was supposed to do a water healing that day, though I literally had no idea what a water healing even was. I just knew that I had to do it. I was raised Methodist, and the Pentecostal "baptism in the local creek" thing was as foreign to me as an indigenous tribe in the heart of Africa. I had never even seen one done, except maybe on a television episode of *The Waltons.*

The woofing Cosmic Freight Train sensation had returned even stronger than I had felt it earlier that morning. I wobbled and could barely even stand straight up. Just as my friend Richard Shulman began to play beautiful, meditative piano behind me as an accompaniment, I picked up my bowl of blessed water and stepped in front of a woman inside the circle. I dipped my fingers into the cold water and raised my hand above her head as the blessed water streamed through my fingers onto the top of her head and down across her face.

She began to cry as we looked deeply into each other's eyes. I rested my hand on her forehead and took a deep, cleansing breath as what felt like an immense bolt of lightning shot up through the earth, up through the soles of my feet, through my body, and out the palm of my hand into her third eye as she began to tremble and sway, bursting into tears. The surging continued for several seconds before I felt it run its course and I again went totally empty, much like what had happened onstage a few hours earlier.

I leaned forward and embraced her in my arms, much as my mother did with me when I was feeling overwhelmed with the world as a child. Maybe it was because I had fallen off of my bike and skinned my knee, though it was often brought on by the intense teasing and bullying that my sister and I would often experience on the school bus from a local boy who lived around the corner from our home. I just held her in my arms and became this woman's grounding rod, allowing her to fully feel whatever was moving through her body temple in that moment. She held on for dear life and sobbed openly in my arms.

After holding her for half a minute or so, I stayed fully present in the moment and moved left to the next woman. As soon as our eyes met, she immediately burst into tears and dropped straight down to the ground. I hadn't even placed my hand in the water yet! I continued through all one hundred or so people until well over and hour later, I stood in the center of the room and surveyed what looked like a battlefield of love. Bodies were strewn all over the floor, some still flailing about as if they had a finger pressed into a great cosmic power outlet or light socket, recalibrating them back to the deepest truth of their being.

I felt my inner critic in the back of my mind "*Hoffman, you don't have even the slightest clue what the hell is going on right now, do you?*" I had to admit that, no, I most definitely did not. In ancient Aramaic, the inner critic was called *aaqilqartsa*, which is most often translated as the "*tempter*", "*accuser*" or "*resister*." It is also at time mistakenly translated as "*devil*" or "*satan*". All of these façades thrive within the veils of our own ego – our "*Edging God Out*" – or what Eckhart Tolle calls our "*pain body*".

Aaqilqartsa is the little pitch forked devil on our shoulder, telling us that we are not good enough, not smart enough or completely, irreparably clueless. I felt that inner critic dozens of times that day and I do occasionally, though rarely, hear it from time to time even now during a water blessing, anointing or healing. "*Is this REALLY happening or is it all just all in our heads?*" During my water healings now, however, I much more often hear the words "*Dale, THIS is why you are here on earth, right now, in this very moment! This is your Eternal Path of Light.*"

I soon became enamored with Lonnie Frisbee, also known as "*the hippie preacher*," who also learned to embrace the inherent vulnerability of his own temple through the process of allowing others to feel theirs. I believe that it was Lonnie's utter humility in his healing work that allowed him to be such a powerful vessel for the healing of others. In the late 1960s and early 70s, Lonnie was a huge and primary catalyst in the rapid expansion of a leading Baptist church across North America, only to be essentially chewed up and spit out when they realized that he was homosexual.

Homosexuality is clearly not in any way a religious or political issue. It is purely an issue of *basic, essential human rights*. It is time for those who espouse the teachings of Jesus to once and for all step up and *live it.* Along with fearful, homophobic bullying, pseudo-Christians have long propagated racism, slavery, war, political genocide and even barbaric human torture, backed up and fortified by gross, hateful misrepresentations of religious teachings to condone, support and intensify the absolute most wretched of human evils. I, for one, will not stand by idly, remain mute and allow this to continue. I choose to love.

When we mistake our own unprocessed inner emotional turmoil and darkness to be "*the will of God*," then we have literally become a walking, talking human anti-Christ. We have yet again killed the highest virtues of those who have come to teach us to "*love one another as I have loved you.*" It is time for us to either live it, hand in hand, or to step to the back of the line right now. That tempting little devil on my shoulder is the projection of my own hidden darkness. I need to take responsibility and own it.

I am also so beautifully amused by Yeshua's truth of "*That which you find at fault within another, YOU are guilty of practicing.*" So, when I hear a judgmental preacher screaming homophobic slurs on a Sunday morning telecast, I can see very clearly who it is that he is lashing out at. If he did not have its root within himself, then he would not even feel that hostility and fear which he is now projecting onto his Eternal brother or sister before him. This is the Law of Resonance. In the words of Dr. Ryce, "*If something has happened to you eighty-seven different times with forty-two different people, then who was the ONLY person who was there every time.*" Yes, it is *YOU.*

In my own life, I have learned over time to let all of my inner voices be heard, yet I no longer yield to the ones that do not feel all that good. I bring them forward into the light of my awareness, directly into the eternal fires of truth with a smile on my face and the words "*I love you exactly as you are*" on my lips. If they are based in light and truth, they remain, yet somehow strengthened and recalibrated to the light of Absolute Truth. If they are not real, they simply dissolve. What is real does not die with the body, because what is real is not bound within the constraints of time, space and matter. "*Now that I have let you go, you can return home.*"

Two days after my "pure heart God experience" in Asheville, I was at my beautiful mother's bedside, holding her hand in mine. Cancer had fully consumed almost her entire body and she was little more than a tiny, fading echo of the once strong, fiery dynamo that I knew as my mother. She had softball sized tumors on the back of her head, in her side, on her back, and smaller ones scattered across the rest of her body. Mom could barely speak at all and her communication had been reduced to little more than weakly humming very basic sounds.

After sitting beside my mom for several hours that evening, I let her know that I would be back first thing in the morning. She was able to barely open her eyes into a squint as I held her face in my hands and told her that I loved her so much. I had a very strong feeling that this would be the last time that I would ever look into my mother's human eyes.

The next morning, I was again at mom's bedside. The change in her overnight was unmistakable. Her breathing had become labored and she could no longer open her eyes. I recognized the similarities between mom's breath and that of the Stillpoint Breathing process that I had learned through Dr. Michael Ryce's teachings. I had spent much of the past two decades practicing and teaching Stillpoint Breathing to others to help them process through true healing in their own lives. My mother was breathing this way naturally in her final hours on earth.

I remembered that someone had recently suggested that I climb up into bed with my mother and hold her in my arms, so I did. Her body was so tiny and almost weightless, covered in tumors. I realized that she was very weakly humming "*mmmmmmmm,*" so I began to hum along with her. *"Mmmmmmmm"*

The "m" sound in Aramaic, the letter *mem,* means "water", "flowing", "vast expanse" and "source". I became aware of the flowing water of the birth of my children. Our youngest child, *Shemaya*, would not be born for several more years, though I very distinctly remember the experience of my wife's water breaking for both Lucynda, our oldest, and Mikey, our middle child. I remember making that call to my mother immediately after Lucynda's birth – *"Mom, she's here!"*

This time, I felt like I was saying this very same thing to our ancestors through the humming of the sound *"mmmmmmmm."* I was tearfully announcing my mother's arrival in the next realm back to her mother Irene and father George, as well as her sisters and brothers, friends, family and her entire lineage and beyond. My beautiful mother Ruth was on her way back home, surfing the leading edge of the cosmos. My awareness kept bouncing between the birth of my children and the present moment of my mother's final page in this incarnate chapter. My vision echoed back to the ecstatic state of my mother's being when she first saw Lucynda's little face in person at the Tampa airport eight years earlier as I thought of that group of souls awaiting my mother's arrival in much the same way.

Then, without even making any choice about it, I found myself quietly singing one of my mother's favorite songs, *The Rose – "Sometimes love, it is a river…"* I held her in my arms, breathing, singing, toning and gently rocking her back and forth for over an hour. I embraced her tiny shell of this passing human life and held my mother the way that she held me after a long, exhausting family road trip when I was a child. She would wrap her open, loving arms around my tiny frame as she wiped away my tears, assuring me that *"Everything is going to be okay sweetie. We'll be home soon."*

I held mom in my arms while continually repeating the phrase *"tey tey malkoota"*, *"tey tey malkoota"* – *"thy kingdom come"* – over and over. I felt the overwhelming wave of that Cosmic Freight Train energy that had flooded through me in Asheville three days earlier as I cradled her in my arms. I continued to hum, sing, tone and breathe with her for several hours until an overwhelming feeling arose deep within me that I needed to leave, that she did not want me to see what was about to happen. I carefully laid my mother down in her bed and sat back down in my seat, facing her. I again held her face in my hands and told her *"It has been my absolute highest honor to be your son in this life. I love you."*

And then I heard words coming out of my mouth in an experience that still shakes me to the core of my soul to this day. They just came out.

"Mom, it's okay to let go, because you can only fall back into God."

I kissed mom on her forehead and I left. I never saw my mother alive again. The true jewel of the experience of my mother's passing is that I don't look back on it as only a painful experience so much as a tremendously beautiful one – the gorgeously rich melancholy of an open and real human experience. What an honor it is to know that I was able to be there for my mother in her final hours. I was able to hold love conscious, active and present in an experience that could very easily have been so traumatic for me that I would not have been able to be fully present enough to consciously be with her in that open space as she slipped through the open door between dimensions of reality and back to her eternal home.

What greater honor could I possibly imagine? I held my dear mother in her final human hours just as she held me in my first human hours here on earth. If it had not been for my practice of being aware of the rise and fall of both my own and my mother's breath, as well as toning simple sounds as an avenue for tuning more deeply into the rich experience of the present moment, I would definitely not have been able to hold that space for her.

It was my spiritual path, my willingness to walk directly into the wilderness of the raw edges of my soul that have empowered me to be so wholly alive and conscious at the center of a deeply painful experience.

I had stayed true in my commitment to my spiritual growth and in that willingness to fully feel my own pain, I allowed my mother the freedom to let go of hers.

"Language enfolds reality. We need maps if we are to navigate within a world of energies and powers. We need the power inherent in sacred languages if we are to meet the Keepers of the animals; come into contact with the beings that animate rocks, trees, and stars; and enter the ancient times when alliances and relationships were established by the Grandfathers.

This could also explain why people in the West who spontaneously enter such states experience such great distress. Unable to function effectively in this world, and not knowing the techniques of return, they are considered mad. Such people have wandered into unexplored realms of reality without the maps and language that would help them to contain their experiences. They are devoid of any social context in which to undertake their journey and have never gained the discipline of mind and body that derives from a long process of coming-to-knowing."

F. DAVID PEAT
From the book "*Blackfoot Physics*"
[Weiser Books]

CHAPTER 4

THE REED FLUTE MEETS THE HEART OF THE IRON HORSE

I had many experiences of toning as a child, decades before I ever knew what that meant or that I was even toning. Somehow, even at the age of seven, I knew that the world that I saw all around me was threaded together by sound, vibration and light. I spent almost all of my day outside, either deep in the woods or sitting in my personal nook in the enormous maple tree overlooking my back yard. I would sit high up in the tree for hours, my arms wrapped around her as I breathed in her love and support, especially during times when I felt overwhelmed by the pain and confusion of the world.

Nature was my refuge. The trees were my brothers and sisters and the flowing water of our trickling stream was the breath in my lungs. I often spent hours sitting absolutely still on a fallen tree in a clearing deep in the woods behind our neighbor's farm. I would sit unmoving in vigilant silence, waiting for an animal to wander into the clearing. I yearned to observe nature in her natural state, unaware of human civilization encroaching on her from all directions. I would sit on the earth, toning sounds, an *ahhhhhh* or an *ohhhhhh* for several minutes at a time, just because I liked the way it felt. I especially loved the "echo" that lingered throughout my body after I stopped making the sound.

These forays into the wilderness quickly became the central theme in my life. The natural world was my sanctuary in those moments when I felt that I was being gutted from the inside out during my parents' bitter divorce when I was five years old. I would often just sit and breathe. No technique, no religion, no overarching philosophy. Just a 1970s American kid trying to get a handle on life. I yearned to feel that I had a home that I could count on – a home that would always be there. An eternal home that would wrap me in its loving embrace.

My time outside in the woods had become so healing for me, so full of absolute contentment, that I developed a strong disinterest in the "world of people", even at the age of five. I didn't care about all of the competition, all of the battles. The Vietnam War had just ended two years earlier and, though I wasn't quite sure yet what war was, the one thing that I did know was that it involved competition, suffering, killing, and families being torn apart – and I wanted nothing to do with it.

My refusal to play the stupid games of the world ultimately developed into an extreme empathy to embrace anyone and anything that was suffering. I saw that cruelty and lack of caring so obviously in the hearts of so many of the world's inhabitants, and I began to lash out against it. I wanted to stay within the world's heart. I wanted to stay in nature and the beauty of mother earth. I would have lived in a shelter in the woods if I had been allowed to. It wasn't so much the suffering that bothered me. It was what I perceived as the apathy and utter lack of caring amongst the people who should be holding onto each other for dear life. I had no road map and so had no idea where to turn to escape the pain. So I turned back to nature.

My angered outbursts would eventually be written off as "Dale's bad temper." And so I was labeled. I was a "passionate" kid with sudden temper tantrums. From my view, I just wanted to be seen. *Really* seen. I wanted to hear that everything was going to be okay, that no matter what happened, my home would always be there. But everything wasn't okay. That I knew. I wanted someone to place their hand on my chest and to feel the beating of my heart, to know that I was *really alive*.

One of my favorite summer pastimes was to meander through the peach and sour cherry orchard behind my home and sit on the train tracks, waiting for the afternoon freight line to buzz by. I would grip one rail with both hands and sense the *thump thump* as cars would pass over the tracks on the roads that were a few hundred yards away in either direction.

Every few minutes, I would lay down flat on my belly, merging the length of my body with the mound of filthy earth beneath the railway and set my ear down against an iron rail. I would lie silent and unmoving, feeling little more than the beat of my heart and the rise and fall of my breath. I knew that if I could allow myself to be absolutely still, I could sense the subtle hum of approaching trains, still miles away. I was very aware that this hum was sensed more than heard.

One blazing hot afternoon in the summer of 1980, I cupped my left hand around my mouth and then pressed my hand against one of the rails. Then I started to make a deep sound of *"ahhhhhhhhh"* into the rail while trying to sense the vibration of that tone through the tips of my finger pressed against the rail at arm's length away from my face. I could feel just the slightest sensation of a buzzing in the tips of my fingers.

Then I laid my heart directly on a rail and stretched my arms straight out to either side in an attempt to see if I could feel the beat of my heart through the tips of my fingers pressed against the shining hot metal. I couldn't seem to feel it through the static bar and after some time I came to the conclusion that my beating heart was so obviously *inside* of me that I was not able to put myself outside of my body enough to be able to *observe* it. For the first time in my life, I realized that simply bringing my attention to my hands allowed me to sense and even hear the wheezing pulse of my blood through the tips of my fingers as well as throughout my entire circulatory system. I still use this awareness in my adult life.

The next afternoon was thick, muggy and humid. A loud, crashing thunderstorm had barreled its way through the countryside, temporarily washing away the relentless intensity of the 85-degree midday sun and leaving behind a mucky, sticky mess in its wake. This day, I had brought along my best friend David, enlisting him as an active participant in my heart on the rail experiment. We ran through the muddy orchard at top speed toward the train tracks. I had the possibly brilliant idea that maybe if his heart was beating heavy and strong enough after some intense running, that I would be able to feel its pulse a few feet down the rail a bit easier.

David reluctantly laid down in the slop and pressed his pounding heart against the rail. I moved about five feet down the line and pressed my right ear against the iron while plugging my left ear with a finger. Instantaneously, I heard David's heart beating through the metal. I nodded in satisfaction and moved another five feet away. I couldn't hear it. I instinctively let myself become very still, completely open to the experience. And then it happened. *I felt it*. I *felt* David's heart beating into my ear through the track from ten feet away. I screamed out *"I can even feel it from ten feet away!"*

Just then we heard a train whistle screaming in the distance. We both pressed an ear down on the track and listened as the train began to approach over the next few minutes. The humming vibrations continued to get louder and louder until the huge locomotive rolled around the bend a quarter mile to the east of us. The iron horse thundered toward us with its headlight piercing straight through even the intensity of the blazing midsummer sun. I grabbed a penny out of the side pocket of my faded, mud-splattered jeans and laid it down on the track as we both took a few steps back.

David and I were flapping our arms wildly in the air as the train approached and began passing by us. The conductor waved back and yanked on the whistle twice in acknowledgement – *Toot! Tooooooot!* We stood there, no more than 10 feet away from the passing rail cars, smiles wide on our faces, as the power of the sour diesel-tinged air shot straight up our noses and forced us back away from the tracks, the earth quaking and rumbling beneath our feet. As soon as the caboose passed us, we both ran to the tracks to locate the penny. There it was, smashed flatter than a dime. I gave it to David, a minor reward for a job well done. We kneeled down and held on the rails with both hands as the echoing rumble diminished into a droning hum before trailing off back into the silence.

Years later, in my late teens, Dee Brown's epic and at times heartbreaking tome *Bury My Heart at Wounded Knee* became a wholly consuming fire that burned its bittersweet and yet somehow beautiful light through my soul. It was while reading this much more historically accurate rendering of the ethnic genocide of the native peoples of what would become the American continent that I experienced a very hair raising realization about my childhood experiments in yearning to sense a natural heartbeat through the "backbone of the iron horse."

It was this very nineteenth century "iron internet" that transported soldiers, 49ers, mountain men, "beaver eaters" and more than a few Euro-Americans demanding their "manifest destiny" as shareholders of the "American Dream" across the "new" lands. These rails also brought out untold thousands of hunters and buffalo poachers with the sole intent of wiping out the *tatanka* – the buffalo – the living heart of the plains nations, in the hope that those very nations could be forced into surrender to their own "obvious" destiny, at least in the eyes of the self-proclaimed superior and "civilized" white man. They wanted to strip them away from their true home, the land of their ancestors in untold generations before them. The deeper archetype of my childhood seeking to sense the pulse of a human heart coursing through the iron rail is not lost on me.

To this day, I still have an almost rapturous fascination with trains that I feel mildly amuses my wife and children. The sound of the wailing whistle still beckons me further; far beyond the outermost reaches of what we label "civilization;" far beyond the fringe of what is "proper" and deeper into the dark-light womb of the mother. I read of that longing in the books of Laura Ingalls Wilder, Jack London and Jack Kerouac. I hear that longing through the music of Woody Guthrie, Pete Seeger, Hank Williams, Johnny Cash and John Gorka, among many others. It is such a lonesome, yet somehow richly nourishing tone that feels like a healing balm on the wounds of my ancient heart. It is like the tranquility bell of a Buddhist monastery, bringing me fully into the present moment, back into the profound emptiness of my open heart, back to the natural rhythm of my breath receding back into the stillness of the unbroken shadows of my being.

I may very likely have been a hobo in a previous incarnation, or maybe a traveling minstrel. Could it be that I may have been a snake oil salesman or possibly even one of those imminent manifest destiny blokes? Possibly a humble, yet absolutely fearless warrior? I have never done much of any intensive investigation into my past lives because in truth I have never really cared all that much about who I *was*. I care about who *I AM*. Right here, right now, in this present moment. And who I am is deeply moved by the sound of a moaning train whistle.

Rumi's poetry spoke of the mournful, longing sound of the reed flute having been plucked from its natural home in the marsh. The sound of the flute fashioned from the reed is the yearning, lonesome sound of a soul that seeks to return to its true home, to its eternal nature. I recognized that sound deep within myself, though it would be many years before I would know exactly what that longing was. I recognized that longing in the primordial howl of the train whistle and many years later in the primal cries of my children after their birth.

That almost primal, if manmade, wail returns me to those starless nights back in the late '70s when I would fall asleep with the earphone of my hand held transistor radio given to me by my great-grandfather pressed into my ear. I was taking in the sounds of the Philadelphia am radio stations broadcasting from just across the Delaware River and would often drift off to sleep to the sounds of hockey and baseball games, or more often '50s rock and roll music. I would envision the radio waves dancing in expanding circles through the air across the countryside and diving headfirst into my little box.

That whistle takes me back to 2am, when the battery on my transistor radio had long since petered out, as that serpentine, fire breathing dragon rolled its way past my boyhood home. Back to those black as coal nights when the only visible light in the sky was blazing forth from the glowing halo at the head of that chugging locomotive on its way to the ultimate realization of a mission completed, a job well done. Welcome home prodigal One. *I see you.*

"The earth is such a powerful metaphor for truth that vision questers will dig a hole in the earth and go down into the hole to be more in tune with that silence fused with perfection. It is not surprising then that the chambers for teaching the ancient mysteries were underground. Going underground was the metaphor for entering the perfected self.

As a young boy, I was taught in those underground chambers to look within. I discovered I was silence and darkness. And then I saw that by seeing with my eyes I created movement and out of it illumination came, and then I realized the silence and darkness were full of emptiness, and the emptiness was full of light."

JOSEPH RAEL
From the book "*Being and Vibration*"
[Millichap 2015 Edition]

CHAPTER 5

THE TUNNEL OF STREAMING LIGHT

After decades of observing the transformative powers of vibration and sound on consciousness, I still grin when I think of how we birth into this dimension of human existence, so obviously pre-wired with the naturally intuitive capacities for using sound and vibration to heal and shift our state of awareness. We just seem to come in already "knowing." However, for those of being raised in "civilized" societies, much of this innate sensitivity is often pummeled out of us, piled beneath bushel baskets full of religious indoctrination and an educational system built upon the culturally rewarded value of memorization rather than an eternal truth of cultivating and openly expressing sacred insight and perception.

In his book *Magical Child*, Joseph Chilton Pearce reveals that the one common denominator possessed by adult geniuses is that they were allowed an abundance of "staring out into space" time as a child. It is in fact not the rote memorization and conditioning of information, but rather the cultivation of *observation and perception* that allows a child to flower fully. In fact, the latin root sound *educare* means to "*draw out the essence of, to foster growth and to bring up*".

I spent the vast majority of my childhood up to the age of ten outside, most often deep in the woods surrounding my home. My young life was so deeply threaded into nature and the earth that I began at a very early age to say a silent prayer and blessing when I would encounter a dead animal. Whether I was on a four hour road trip with my family, or a five minute trip to the local market, I would always say a prayer for each and every lifeless animal that we would pass on the side of the road.

I also allowed my mother the common thrill of finding creative new ways to extract dirt and muck from my clothes, not to mention slithering snakes from my pockets after a day of exploring. Above all else, I was almost always barefoot, which my mother was not all that supportive of. "*Dale Allen, you have to wear your shoes if you are going out into the woods*" was my mother's daily spoken rite.

"*I will mom*" was my standard response.

I would exit the house with my shoes on and, as soon as I was within the boundary of the woods, I would take my shoes off and stash them under a growth of skunk cabbage. *Done!* Still to this day, I almost never wear shoes unless I have to. I will never speak or offer teachings with something covering my feet. I need to feel the earth beneath my feet, even if that means the cheap carpet on the 27th floor of a building. The voice of eternity is still present on the 27th floor just as well as it is at the ground level of our being, but only if you can allow yourself to be open enough to sense her subtle, feminine voice.

I am often amused at how offensive some of the "old guard" at many churches judge this to be. Some even stand up and walk out of the room when I walk in barefoot, smelling like essential oils and looking like I jumped out of Haight-Ashbury during the summer of 1967. I am often quick to point out that this judgment of "*one must wear shoes at a public gathering*" is in fact not anti-intuitive, as they espouse, but rather *anti-conditioning.*

Thich Nhat Hanh, one of the original inspirations of my early 1990s awakening, shares in his teachings on walking meditation for us to step mindfully as we imagine our feet kissing and massaging the backbone of mother earth. My holy relationship with the earth and being barefoot continues well into midlife for me. Nurturing and refining my awareness of this natural bioelectric relationship of vibration and consciousness between my human energy system and the fertile, rooted earth beneath my feet has been of immeasurable value to me as I continue to mature and ripen in my life.

It was not until a decade ago when raw and living foods advocate David Wolfe told me as we both stood barefoot beside the raging whitewater of the French Broad River in Hot Springs, North Carolina that I realized the health benefits of being barefoot. I began to piece together the science behind my habit when he told me that the human body seeks an electrical ground through the soles of its feet every ninety seconds. If the body does not find that ground, it instantaneously enters into a state of biological stress, which is then compounded every ninety seconds if that ground is not realized.

Of course the "*earthing*" movement has been in existence for some time now, but has really begun to thrive in our more recent aspirations to return our awareness to our innate relationship with our earth mother through whom we have been borne forth. We seek more natural ways of living in harmony with all of life and its many appearances of manifestation. I see that love of barefoot walking has been passed down to both of my daughters, Lucynda and Shemaya, as neither of them has much use for shoes.

As a child I would often walk barefoot down the hill from my home to the stream bordering my yard while trying to remain as still as I could, even in the process of walking, aware of my feet massaging the cool patches of young, bright green grass beside the cool water. I would then step into the stream and very slowly sit down, then lay back with my head resting on a sandbar. I would be almost completely submerged, with only my nose and mouth above the water, aware of how my maternal grandmother Irene often referred to the drops of rain that flow into this stream as "the tears of angels in heaven."

After several minutes of lying nearly immobile, I would begin gently humming "*mmmmmmmmm,*" enveloped in the cocoon of reflections and echoes through the water and back into my skin. I would often lay flat in the water for an hour or more at a time, feeling out different sounds and comparing the various qualities and feelings that each sound evoked within me as I made them.

"*ahhhhhhhhhhhhh*"

"*oooooooooooooo*"

"*eeeeeeeeeeeeeeee*"

I loved to climb into the underground irrigation tunnel that allowed the stream to flow under our road and down into the pastureland of the farm across the street from us. The huge, discolored dark steel tube was a great laboratory for my experiments in the relationship between the sounds I made, the sounds I heard around me, and the feelings these experiences evoked within me. The ridged surface of the heavy steel tube gifted me with infinite layers of echoing reflections as my voice returned to me in a symphony of disorienting, yet nurturing chaos.

Today, I feel so deeply grateful for this fascination with the relationship between sounds and consciousness that I was dabbling in even as a child. I wasn't thinking about it in any technical way at all back then though. I didn't really care *why* it worked. I just loved the way it *felt*, especially in my subterranean sound chamber. I was as equally fascinated with the multitude of echoes as I was with the distinct character and timbre of personality which each echo seemed to embody as they reflected back into my awareness of perception.

Even though I knew that I was in truth only hearing my own voice, the rich layers of what sounded like a choir of hundreds of unique and distinct personas was so easy to lose my self-awareness within. It did not require much imagination to suspend my knowing, often unconsciously, that these were merely reverberations of my own voice. I would feel as if I were in relationship with a panoply of separate, individually conscious voices crying out in the darkness of my cave.

In his almost two and a half-thousand-year-old text *The Republic*, Plato likened the experience of enlightenment, or the lack thereof, with a group of human beings chained up and immobilized within a dark den beneath the surface of the earth. Unable to move their heads and bodies about due to the heavy chains which bound them to the earth, they were unable to observe their own bodies or those of their companions. Each human was only able to see the shadows of themselves and each other cast on the walls of the cave by a fire which was blazing above and behind them.

They would also see the shadows of other beings entering from outside the mouth of the cave who would walk across a raised path behind them. Plato wrote of how, without the ability to be aware of the reflection of self, we can so easily mistake the voices which enter from the light apparently *outside* the cave of our unconsciousness as being what is real. These infinite chorales of seemingly separate and distinct voices are in truth simply crystalline, prismatic refractions of the one, undivided eternal voice of Life Itself.

In his beautifully eloquent, deeply mystical book *Being and Vibration*, Joseph Rael, aka *Tslew-teh-koyeh* or *Beautiful Painted Arrow*, wrote of his boyhood experiences of walking through his Picuris Pueblo village near Taos, New Mexico, seeking to blur the subjective lines between his human senses. He would seek to tune into and awaken his relationship with the mental, emotional and spiritual energies all around him, whether they were within his realm of awareness and sensitivity in that moment or not.

In the summer of 1983, Joseph was sun dancing when the vision of a man appeared before him. The man moved toward Joseph and then suddenly disappeared as an oval shaped, kiva-like chamber appeared in the earth where the man had been standing moments before. The chamber was filled with men and women singing. Joseph, knowing that what we recognize as our personal "self" is but an echo of the eternal Vast Self, saw that these sound chambers would resonate a key ingredient in the physical, planetary and environmental well-being of humanity and our earth mother. Now over three decades later, Joseph has inspired and facilitated in the birthing of peace chambers for toning and prayer all across the earth.

My experiences deep within the earth in my "toning tunnel" helped to awaken an awareness within me of the very subtle, feminine, flowing and less concrete qualities of the sounds and vibrations of the world we are walking through in our brief parentheses here on earth. It has been this awareness that has drawn me ever forward in my quest to comprehend the richly fertile layers of insight and nuance embedded within the very sounds that we often spit out absent mindedly thousands of times over in the course of our day. I am not satisfied with resting on the "facts" of the common, everyday meanings of the words that we use. I want to know what my ancestors – my ancient brothers and sisters – *felt* about the most basic tones and vibrations that we have built our many thousands of languages upon over the passing threads of millennia.

It was this vision within my own heart, awakened from deep within the sacred womb of our mother earth that has brought me to this place that I am at the time of this writing in the summer of the 2014. It is now a quarter of a century after my childhood experiences of toning in the embrace of a flowing country stream and in an underground steel tunnel surrounded by the fertile earth. Now in my fourth decade of this human incarnation, I still continue to evolve into a deeper understanding of what I felt as a child. I realize now that these experiences were not about me "understanding" them so much as they happened to create a fertile base for standing under the extraordinary life that I was about to live here on earth.

"What's the eye behind the I?
I Am
Who's the me behind the eye
through which I see?
Am I the watcher?
Or is there something else
that's wanting to be seen
....through me?"

BOB SIMA
"*I Am*"
[From the album *putalittlemoreloveintheworld*]

CHAPTER 6

BIRTHING HEAVEN THROUGH ANCIENT TONES

The deeper I journey into the nuance and depth of meaning of ancient texts and teachings, the more profoundly I am struck by their veiled subtlety of wisdom that is virtually invisible to the naked, worldly human eye. The less tangible, less clearly defined and much more feminine experiential qualities of these cosmic insights allow themselves to be seen only when we allow them to flow through our being, unimpeded by the artificially limited intellectual concepts of only what our thinking mind can comprehend. When I allow myself to *feel* with my heart, rather than to simply comprehend with my mind, I activate a depth of direct experience that I so often cannot even begin to express with obvious words.

I have learned that a clear definition does not need to precede a deeply profound spiritual experience or state of being in any way whatsoever. An agreed upon definition can at times be a signpost, but it can also in many ways restrict the very breadth of experience that reveals herself only through a fully present moment of absolute openness. Our need for labeling a word, phrase or experience with the restrictive judgments of accepted definitions can keep the intensity of our mental focus upon the words themselves rather than the space *between* the words, where the Gnostic truth of direct experiential mystery silently resides. I am learning to allow myself to feel without needing to comprehend exactly what may or may not be happening in any moment.

I heard someone say once that if you feel good, you're in heaven. If you don't feel good, you're in hell. While I find that to be a quite cute, if not a bit shallow, belief to hang my hat on, I have always known that there is most definitely more to heaven than feeling good or dropping dead. My realization and intimate recognition of heaven through the richness of my human experience continues to grow on a daily basis.

The most profound example of this for me was the birth of my youngest daughter *Shemaya.* I had a very profound lesson in the magnitude of the vibratory power of the Aramaic language that goes far beyond anything I would ever be able to find in a book, no matter if I searched on and on for eternity. My daughter's name, *Shemaya*, is the Aramaic word for "*heaven,*" as well as "*sky*" or "*vast expanse.*" *Ouranos* is the Greek word for "*the heavens*" or "*cosmic expanse.*"

The *aya* sound at the end of *shemaya* means "*no physical boundary,*" "*no beginning and ending,*" or "*always growing,*" much like a vine. Of course, this double meaning of shemaya reveals how, if we are honest with ourselves, we think of heaven as somehow located in the sky – *it was the very same word!* Shemaya in the heavenly sense is more of an experience that is *felt* rather than any kind of location or place. My youngest child revealed this to me through an experience that I would never even attempt to demean by trying to somehow define it, though I will do my best to relay the story of her arrival.

It was late Thursday morning May 19, 2011 and my wife had been in labor for four days. After some walking around downtown Asheville and a quick bite at a vegan restaurant, we were headed back to our car to drive to an appointment at our midwife's office. Though Loretta's contractions had been coming steadily since Monday, they still had not increased in intensity or fallen into any regularity yet. Hurry up and wait.

As we left the restaurant, we immediately ran into our friend Toni Toney, a pioneer in the raw and living foods movement, specifically in relation to the *ph* balance of the human body. Loretta and I found it beautifully fitting that we had run into Toni, whose work focuses on a beautiful theme of *heaven* and a positive radiating forth from within a body temple that is in a healthy, alkaline *ph.* On the other hand, a body in a more acidic ph could be considered a temple that is experiencing *hell.* To unexpectedly run into Toni was an affirmation for us that "*today is the day*" for heaven's arrival.

When we arrived at the midwives' office, a midwife in training kept Loretta hooked up to all kinds of monitoring machines for well over an hour and then decided it would be a good idea to scrape her membrane in an attempt to stimulate the birth. That is when *all heaven broke loose.*

The contractions immediately intensified to a fevered pitch and started coming full on, less than a minute apart. Loretta was in severe pain and we knew we had to get to the hospital immediately. The office called ahead as we drove out of the parking lot and straight into a traffic jam. We eventually made it to the hospital while I simultaneously tried to make the few alerting phone calls that I had to make. Loretta was rushed up to a room in a wheelchair while I parked the car and I made it up to her room about four minutes later to hear Loretta saying:

"Is my husband here yet? I am not pushing until he is here!"

I said *"I am here."*

The nurses said *"Push!"*

Shemaya launched herself into my hands less than 60 seconds after I had entered the birthing room, still in her full amniotic sac, which was partially torn, though still somehow mostly intact. It had been a decade since the birth of our two older children, so I didn't notice anything that seemed to be out of the ordinary. I was elated and buzzing with the anticipation of an expectant father.

Our dear friend Dr. Barbara Waterhouse of the Center for Spiritual Living in Asheville came into the room just as I stood back and one of the nurses began to peel a thin veil back away from Shemaya's face. I was so thrilled that I had no idea that something rather unique was unfolding before our eyes as one of the nurses said *"She's born in the caul!"*

Barbara said *"Dale that's really rare!"*

"The call?" I said.

The nurse responded *"The caul, C – A – U – L." It means that she was born with the veil still across her face, and even in her amniotic sac, which is even rarer."*

I still had no idea what she meant as she continued, *"We really don't keep track of this kind of birth so we aren't even sure how rare it is,"* as she gently cleared out Shemaya's mouth and nose with a syringe.

That's when it hit me that Shemaya was not crying, and I knew that was usually not a good sign, though she seemed to be very alert as they laid her on Loretta's chest. The room was absolutely electric with the vibration of an immense breathing light and the emanating peace of this stunningly beautiful newborn angel.

"Oh. My. God. Who does she look like?" I said to my wife.

"That is your mother!" she replied.

Her face looked exactly like my dear mother Ruth, who we had lost to her very intense battle with cancer just three and a half years before. Shemaya lay on Loretta's chest as Barbara and I embraced each other. After a few minutes a nurse lifted Shemaya away from Loretta to take her measurements and weight. Shemaya instantaneously let loose a wailing scream that could probably be heard in Eastern Europe.

As soon as the nurse laid Shemaya on the scale, she peed all over the place as the nurse said "*Well, we know that works!*" but Shemaya kept screaming. I knew that screaming was a good thing that would help clear her lungs and airway, though this scream felt less like a natural cry of *"I am alive!"* and more like *"Leave me alone, I want my mother!"*

I slowly reached my hand toward Shemaya and she grabbed my right pinky with her entire hand and looked up at me, still crying, though not as intensely. I kneeled down slowly so as not to twist her hand and dropped down to my knees as if I were going to pray and I looked straight into her eyes and toned

"Ahhhhhhbwooon d'bwshmaya!"

Shemaya instantaneously fell silent and gazed straight into my soul as I continued.

"Nitqadash shmakh.

Tey tey malkootak.

Nehway t'sibyanak

Aykana d'bshmaya ahp b'arha"

We were both absolutely enthralled. The room became absolutely still and silent, as if in a state of suspended animation. You could have heard a feather drop in Siberia. Tears flooded into my eyes. The room was electric and pulsating and breathing. Shemaya and I both stayed locked deep into each other's eyes for what felt like eternity.

As with the birth of our children Lucynda and Michael, I felt the recognition of a soul whom I have known since before the dawn of time.

But I had never seen a child so fully present and so focused straight out of the womb. I had never even seen a child less than maybe three or four weeks old with this kind of clear focus and gaze. Since Shemaya's birth I have personally witnessed dozens of babies with this kind of "medically impossible" focus and gaze.

I never had even the slightest regret that Shemaya and her granny Ruth would never get the chance to meet and enjoy each other's presence. Somehow, I immediately knew that my mother held Shemaya before we did. I knew that my mother had already spent considerable time with Shemaya before her birth, lovingly prepping her for this earthly journey to come. In fact, it was only after Maya's third birthday that we noticed her no longer walking hand in hand with her much taller "imaginary" friend and instead began asking *"Where's granny? I don't see her anymore!"* The first time our little one asked this question, every single hair on my body stood straight on end while an affirming smile emerged on my face. *I knew. And I knew that Shemaya knew.*

This knowing has gone hand in hand with my intimate experience of how these Aramaic tones reopened an eternal relationship between my youngest daughter and I while simultaneously reaffirming something I already long known: There is something about the vibrational essence of some languages and consciously toned sounds that goes far beyond the surface level, colloquial and common meanings that they get branded with by those working simply on the level of accepted labels and definitions.

These tones touch on something that is much more naturally cosmic and eternal by its very nature. The inherent power of these ancient sounds is less predicated by perfect or correct physical pronunciation as it is by the clarity of our intentions, goals, and willingness to be open to feel their natural expansion and expression *through us, as us.* It is so very important for each of us to remember and embrace our own, unique relationship with these ancient words and sounds in whatever manner we choose. We can move our awareness toward whatever sounds and tones resonate most deeply for our life journey. It is all a matter of personal choice. Whether you are looking for the scientific study of linguistics or the living, breathing essence of our deepest eternal truths, we must embrace this passion with the wholeness of our hearts.

As I began to move deeper and deeper into the vibratory and healing nature of languages and communication, I began to come into a much deeper experiential relationship with the sounds themselves that ran so much deeper than the much more common meanings that exist on the surface. I began to realize that the Aramaic words *abwoon d'bshmaya*, when consciously toned, awakened a depth of experience that could *never* be constrained by the words *"Our Father who art in Heaven."*

For me, even as early as the age of seven, those King James English words which were spit out so monotonously and vacantly on a Sunday morning held virtually no essential life energy whatsoever. Even as a child, they felt like nothing more than dead platitudes, devoid of any true depth or inherent spark. The pursuit to uncover the essential spark in the Jesus teachings drove me forward in my sacred quest and continues to do so to this very moment. This journey of sound and light continues to carry me ever deeper into an ever-awakening experience of life as vibration – deeper into *"The Word."*

SECTION TWO

THE WORD: *Seeing Beyond the Letters on the Page*

"Words strain, crack and sometimes break, under the burden,
Under the tension, slip, slide, perish,
Decay with imprecision, will not stay in place,
Will not stay still."

T.S. ELIOT
From the book "*The Four Quartets*"
[Mariner Books]

CHAPTER 7

IN THE BEGINNING WAS THE *MILTA*

To get a deeper grasp on the words of and about Yeshua from an experiential perspective, let's go back to the very first line in the beginning of the Aramaic *Gospel of Yokhanan*, aka the Gospel of John. Though these words are not attributed to Yeshua himself, they do embody a richly layered depth of vision in resonance with some of humanity's most sacred spiritual wisdom all the way back to the dawn of recorded philosophy and spiritual insight.

ܒܪܫܝܬ ܐܝܬܘܗܝ ܗܘܐ ܡܠܬܐ

Beresheet aytahwee hwah Milta

I am often asked during radio, television and print interviews: *"What is the most difficult word to get from ancient Aramaic into modern English?"* My answer to that is always the same: *"The Word"*, which usually elicits a laugh and *"No, really! Seriously!"* I *am* being serious! The Aramaic word that is translated as "the Word" in the first line of the Gospel of John is possibly the most multi-faceted, misunderstood and often misrepresented word in the entire New Testament. This realization often brings to mind the apostle Paul, formerly *Saul of Tarsus*, a native Aramaic speaker, who offered this nugget of wisdom in 2 Corinthians 3:6: "*The letter kills but rookha* (*breath – spirit*) *brings forth life*".

Since the ancient Aramaic term *milta* is so impossible to fully translate into modern English, most responsible translators will usually leave the word untranslated. So, in most Aramaic to English translations of this line, you will see *"In the beginning was the Milta"*, which would be accompanied by an in depth commentary that assists the reader in gaining a greater understanding of this very sacred, ancient Aramaic word. In the next chapter of this book, I will unpack some of the much deeper meanings of the word *beresheet*, the first word of the Hebrew Torah as well as the Aramaic Gospel of John translated as "*in the beginning*".

I could write several pages full of English words *about* milta, each of which may embody some aspects of what milta represents, though there is not one English word or even phrase that can contain the wide-ranging scope of this beautiful Aramaic jewel. Milta is derived from, though much greater in depth than the Aramaic word *mela*, which is a word that is simply spoken or written on a page. These spoken or written qualities are simply facets of the prismatic refractions embodied within milta itself.

First, let me give you a few English words and phrases which represent qualities of milta, though no direct word for word translation exists. Before you jump into reading these words, first close your eyes and tune into how your body *feels* from within, right where you are. The position of your body is not very important right now. Notice any sensations or waves of energy and awareness that may be flowing through what the Aramaic Yeshua teachings refer to as our *hykla*, or *energy body*, usually translated as *temple.*

Next, take three full, cleansing breaths into your nose, holding each inward breath for a few moments, and then releasing each exhalation fully through your mouth. After the third breath, allow yourself to be silent and still, fully present in this moment. Then, when you feel present and centered, read these words:

Word • Emanation • Willed Action • Awareness • Secretion
Giving Off • Instance • Occurrence • Outward Flow/Expansion
Matter • Substance • Essence • Meaning • Cause • Story
Subject • Ground-Root-Branch-Fruit • Aspiration • Emergence
Beginning through End • Alef through Taw • Alpha through Omega

Start through Completion • Implicate is Explicate • Manifestation
Expression • Archetype • Prototype • Appearance • Likeness
Torah • Living Law • Consciousness Creating • Utterance
Sound • Depiction • Statement • Expression • Expansion
Declaration • Intention • Goal • Target • Purpose • Phrase
Objective • Affirmation • Announcement • Message • Case
Representation • Account • Report • Story • Tale • Image
Narrative • Description • Testimony • Communication

Can you sense a "common thread" running through these seemingly varied words and phrases? It is this gleaming thread of awareness which runs through the center of these dozens of terms which holds the magic of cultivating "*eyes that see and ears that hear*". *Milta* is the ever subtle, delicate membrane of consciousness which joins together the continuum of the Absolute Ground of Being and Ultimate Creation, between the un-manifest and the manifest. *Milta is consciousness itself!*

We can unpack this continuum of conscious creation even further with the verse Hebrews 11:3 from the Aramaic Khabouris Codex:

ܒܗܝܡܢܘܬܐ ܓܝܪ ܡܣܬܟܠܝܢܢ ܕܐܬܬܩܢܘ ܥܠܡܐ

b'hayyemanoota geyr mestakleenan d'ataqano ealmah

"Through faith we realize that "the world" (*ealmah*)
is brought into form (*ataqano*)

ܒܡܠܬܐ ܕܐܠܗܐ

b'milta d'Alaha

through the "Word" (*milta*) of *Alaha – the Absolute, Only, Being*

ܘܗܠܝܢ ܕܡܬܚܙܝܢ ܗܘܝ

ohaleyn d'metkhazyan hoay

That which is "seen/perceived" (*metkhazyan*)
is already (*hoay*) made of

ܡܢ ܐܝܠܝܢ ܕܠܐ ܡܬܚܙܝܢ

man ahyleyn d'la metkhzeyn

elements (*ahyleyn*) not yet drawn out (*d'la*)

as to be revealed to the [physical] senses"

"The Word" is the original *prototype* or primal *archetype* which organizes and forms the basis for the "world," "reality" or "dream" that we perceive as our "life". It is also the final manifestation and the essential matrix of intelligence which brings about this ultimate manifestation as *one singular, undivided continuum or whole undivided process.* "The Word" is the filmstrip in the projector, the projector and the projection screen as one undivided whole!

For some, this quote may feel a bit out of your realm of comprehension, though I ask that you take another look at it. This time, first take a step back in your awareness, take a breath and allow yourself to return to your center before reading it again. It is in actuality quite clear when one has "*eyes that see and ears that hear*". This is a vital, essential truth in understanding the power of affirmation.

"The Word" is the original prototype or primal archetype which organizes and forms the basis for the "world," "reality" or "dream" that we perceive as our "life". It is also the final manifestation and the essential matrix of intelligence which brings about this ultimate manifestation as one singular, undivided continuum or whole, undivided process."

The word prototype is derived from the Greek *prototypos*, meaning "*original, primal existence or form*". It is a combination of two Greek terms: *protos* meaning "*original*" or "*first*" and *typos* meaning "*essence*", "*impression*" or "*form*". "The Word" is the consciousness or essential filament which threads through the original image or intent as well as its replication or reflected "form". The Word is the essential thread of communication between the "seer" and the "seen", between the initial spark or idea and its ultimate manifestation. In truth, The Word is the original vision, the process of manifestation, as well as the final creation as one singular, whole continuum of being.

One outdated idea that I would love to see us grow and evolve beyond is the idea that "our thoughts create our life," or that "we become what we think about." This is not true in any way, shape or form, except within our perception of what we call "the world" or "our life". It is time for us to mature beyond the erroneous idea that we are the world that we see, or that what we call "our life" is essentially "real" at all, except within our imagination. The most cutting edge quantum science backs up this truth. Our "life" and the "world" are simply our dream, the projection of our thoughts, but it is not our "life."

We are NOT the world that we envision and dream, we are *LIFE ITSELF*. Our thoughts create our *human dream*, which we then mistakenly view as our "life." It is time for us to awaken into the realization of Paramahansa Yogananda's guidance that we learn to see the dualistic scenes of life as "*the ever-joyous witness of a stupendous cosmic drama*". We are the not what we perceive as "the world", but rather we are literally *THE CONSCIOUS LIGHT OF LIFE ITSELF.*

I strongly feel that twentieth century New Thought icon Ernest Holmes may have very well understood the deeper singular, non-dual experiential aspects of biblical Creation teachings and processes more than many of the self-proclaimed prophets of the past 2,000 years. Ernest definitely realized Yeshua's deeper insights much more comprehensively than most biblical or language authorities have ever had even a hope of comprehending in their incessant pursuit of specialized "facts" and "expertise". In his classic 1926 work *The Science of Mind*, Ernest spoke of the "three attributes of spirit" – Spirit, The Word and Law. These three attributes ultimately became the foundation of the wildly popular Religious Science philosophy based on his teachings. Ernest wrote:

"One of the main facts to bear in mind is that of the three attributes of Spirit, The Word alone is conscious of itself. The "Law" is force, and matter is simply stuff ready to take form.... Law is not a thinker but is a doer, while matter cannot think, but is thought upon."

Ernest also wrote: *"The starting point of all creation is in the Word of Spirit. The Word is the Concept, Idea, Image, or Thought of God. It is the Self-Knowing Mind speaking Itself into Manifestation. Everything has a Word back of it as its initial Cause."*

One more succinct quote, this time from the apostle Paul in Romans Chapter 4, sheds even more light on the fertile process of conscious creation in "the Word":

"God, within whom you are being and living, quickens and gives life to the dead or not yet existing, and calls those things which are not, as if they were."

The Word calls things as if they *already were*, and always have been, not as they appear to be right now. Even more important is Paul's declaration that we are within God, rather than petitioning some sort of power or presence outside of our appearance as a separate human "self". Remember, the "kingdom" is everywhere. What we call "God" is in truth the very fiber of All Being Itself! In the words of Plotinus: *"Just as the spoken word is an echo of the thought in the psyche, so thought in the psyche is itself an echo from elsewhere."*

Let's look deeper into some of the linguistic aspects of *milta* from an ancient Aramaic point of view. The *"ta"* sound at the end of *milta* genders the word feminine. What exactly does that mean? Boy and girl? Well, at times, yes, but in the case of *milta*, the truth is much more richly insightful than that.

First, let me explain the ideas of masculine and feminine in terms of language. *Hermeneutics*, or the scientific study of the sounds of languages and how those sounds are brought together to create words of implicit meaning, can unpack the masculine-feminine continuum from the perspective of how letters *sound*. Unfortunately, the scientific study of the implicit meanings embedded *within the sounds themselves* is often pushed aside in favor of the much easier to analyze and debate *conceptual* thought-meanings of words on the common, everyday colloquial level of speech and writing.

For me, language gender is not a clear and fast rule, but rather only a guideline. Virtually all languages that did or still do embody gender are a bit messy in their labels of gender, with Aramaic most definitely included. Language gender can at times be a very slippery slope, with an abundance of disagreements amongst scholars about just how correct or incorrect many word and sound gender labels may be. As with many language characteristics and meanings, few agree. This mess is amplified by the inability to see beyond the everyday, common and widely-accepted definitions which many words are bound within on the limited, though much less challenging surface level.

It is of course much, much easier to study the common, everyday meanings of written words on a page than it is to bring oneself into the much deeper inquiry of the actual *meaning of the base sounds of spoken communication themselves*. Pointing at the moon is not much of a challenge.

Getting to the moon itself, however, poses a much greater commitment and investment of time and energy, doesn't it?

When looking at masculine and feminine from the perspectives of how they *sound*, hard consonants like "k", "d" or "t" would be considered masculine in the quality of their sounds. Vowels, or lighter, less percussive sounds, such as "a", as in "apple", "ee" as in "beet", or "ah" as in "obvious" would be considered more feminine in sound, meaning more open and flowing. In the case of the English letter "y", its use in the word "you" would be considered more masculine, whereas its use in the word "boy", the "y" would be more feminine. *Understand?* In fact, it is for this very reason that we were told in English class that the vowels are "a, e, i, o, u and *sometimes* "y". The "y" is only a part-time vowel because sometimes "y" is pronounced as more of a masculine consonant, whereas at other times it is a much more feminine vowel.

I share this sound quality of masculine and feminine only as a guideline, as this outlook on the feminine, flowing quality of how a letter sounds does not influence its labeled gender. This is only one tiny aspect of the feminine meaning of *milta* because the labeling of a word's gender does not come from its sound, but rather from its accepted *definition.* I wanted to lay the base of the more percussive masculine and more flowing feminine qualities of sounds themselves before I moved on to why *milta* is gendered feminine rather than masculine.

Let me explain: Your *perception* or *observation* of the book or digital device on which you are reading these words right now would be considered *feminine*, whereas the book or device *itself* would be considered *masculine.* In other words, your perception of an object or thing is feminine, yet the object or "*thing*" itself – the Aramaic word *medem* – is masculine. The feminine is an "*experience*", a "*perception*", an "*attitude*", an "*observation*", etc. The masculine is *manifest*, which is derived from the Latin word meaning "*obvious*", or, more accurately, "*as obvious as one's own hand*".

Let's look at another example. If you are sitting in a chair, then your perception of that chair is *feminine* and the actual chair itself is masculine. Got it? Other Aramaic words can help unpack the recognition of feminine versus masculine gender, such as the words *malkoota* and *malkootey*. The *ta* and *ey* sounds at the end of both words genders them *feminine.* Want to guess what this word is translated as in modern English? *Kingdom.*

Even more confusion is pulled into the "kingdom" mix once we learn that the *mem-lamad-kap* tri-consonantal Aramaic and Hebrew *mlk* root sound of "kingdom" did eventually become synonymous with "king" or "ruler" in the earthly sense, a definition which still holds to this day. The original, several millennia old meaning of the *mlk* sound was actually much closer to "*reign*" or "*boundary of influence*" than it was a label for the earthly power of a person. I will uncover a bit more about this aspect later in this book.

The Greek word translated as "*kingdom*" is *basilea*, which is again a *feminine gendered word!* What does this mean? It means that the "*kingdom*" that Yeshua spoke of is not a place or location, but rather a perception, attitude, state of being or direct experience. Of course, this is why he told his listeners in the Coptic Gospel of Thomas that if the kingdom was in the sky, then the birds would get there first. Or if the kingdom, was located in the sea then the fish would precede us. Very simple! The kingdom is not a *masculine* location; it is a *feminine* state of being!

Yeshua expanded upon this truth in his discussion with *Peelatos* – aka *Pontius Pilate* – in John Chapter 18, though it very likely fell upon deaf ears for virtually everyone within earshot at the time, much as it often does today:

ܡܠܟܘܬܝ ܕܝܠܝ ܠܐ ܗܘܬ ܡܢ ܗܢܐ ܥܠܡܐ

Mlkoothey delee lah hoat hanah ealmah

"My *mlkootey* is not "of this world" (*ealmah*).

ܐܠܘ ܡܢ ܥܠܡܐ ܗܘܬ ܗܢܐ ܡܠܟܘܬܝ

aeloo man ealmah hoat hanah mlkoothey

If my *mlkootey* existed within this world,

ܡܬܟܬܫܝܢ ܗܘܘ ܡܫܡܫܢܝ ܕܠܐ ܐܫܬܠܡ ܠܝܗܘܕܝܐ

metktsheen hoao m'shmshany d'lah aeshtlem l'huodayeah

my attendants would have fought
to keep me from being handed over to the Judeans

ܗܫܐ ܕܝܢ ܡܠܟܘܬܝ ܕܝܠܝ ܠܐ ܗܘܬ ܡܟܐ

hashah deyn mlkootey diylee lah hoat mekah
But in this present moment (*hashah*),
my *mlkootey* is not from "here" (*mekah*)"

The Orthodox view of this phrase would simply claim that Yeshua was referring to some sort of promised "kingdom" or "dominion" that exists only after we die, but the Aramaic text does not say any such thing whatsoever. What both of these texts *do* say is that this *mlkootey* that Yeshua is referring to is not located within time or space. It is *not of this "world"*. Why? Because this *mlkootey* is not a masculine location or place but rather a feminine perception, an attitude, a state of being – *a direct "spiritual" experience*. Saying 113 of the Coptic Gospel of Thomas says:

> "His disciples said to Him, "*When will the Kingdom come?*" [Jesus said] "*It will not come by waiting for it. It will not be a matter of saying 'Here it is' or 'There it is.' Rather, the Kingdom of the One is spread out upon the earth, and people do not see* [comprehend] *it.*"

I am not sure how much clearer he could have possibly been, yet many still speak of the "Kingdom" as a masculine place, location or physical region of power and influence rather than a feminine *perception* or *state of being*. It is definitely time for our relationship with the Yeshua teachings to grow up. The moment has come for us to be nakedly honest about what is right there on the page in terms of how do we *live* these teachings through our realization, not how do we fight over them in our ignorance.

Unfortunately, it is so much easier to simply dumb down the avatar teachings of Yeshua to his average contemporary backwater yokel's surface-level meaning or widely-accepted theology. However, this Yeshua character quite obviously came here to crack through these common, widely held ideological beliefs and release them into something much more directly experiential and cosmic in its scope. We will never come into this realization until we let go of our beliefs about the teachings and instead choose to live them directly, from the inside out.

In his native language, Yeshua's teachings were in fact overwhelmingly feminine, meaning that he was speaking of ways of perceiving, feeling and experiencing life much more than he spoke of masculine physical actions, words on a page or ideologies to live up to. Yeshua's teachings are not about our actions, they are about the state of our being – our *presence*, or lack thereof – as we take those actions and consciously create our lives.

Take care the "*heart*". The Aramaic word for heart – *liba* – is not simply the star tetrahedron flesh fractal beating in our chest, but rather the space within our consciousness where our masculine thoughts and our feminine feelings come together in their symbiotic relationship. Living from the space of our heart, not only our physical heart, but from within the depth of conscious presence in this very moment, requires nothing less than the 100 percent commitment. 99.9 percent is not enough. We must live in wholeness to live these insights.

Earlier in Chapter Two, I spoke of my experience at age seven of realizing that I saw the Jesus teaching in Matthew 6 about "*laying up treasures in heaven*" much differently than anyone else in my vacation bible school class, including my teacher. I revealed that I felt very self-conscious that I was somehow not "getting it", since I was the only one who did NOT see heaven as a place that we go to after we die.

Unfortunately, when you are seven years old, you just feel inadequate in those kinds of situations, you feel like a "sore thumb", as if everyone is staring at "the kid who has no clue". It was not until I was 14 years old and suddenly found myself typing page after page of what I call my "riffings" on Jesus' "treasures in heaven" teachings that I realized that I may very well have been seeing more clearly than the others in that room. *Just because a thought pattern, belief or ideology is widespread and commonly accepted definitely does NOT mean that it is accurate!*

The Aramaic word for "treasure" that Yeshua used is *seemta*. Of course the *ta* sound at the end of *seemta* genders this "treasure" that Yeshua is speaking of as *feminine*. He is not speaking of things and stuff that we are getting and stacking up for a post-death place that we are going to, he is speaking of a treasured state of being that is "*spread out upon the earth*" and lives through us right here and right now! He says that where your "*treasure*" is, "*your heart will be also*". When our treasure is in our very presence, our state of being, then our *liba*, or "*heart-continuum*" of thought and feeling, will birth directly from this direct experience as conscious, divine presence as well. This is the very meaning of "*heaven on earth*". Not my human desires, but rather the conscious creation as Life Itself through me, as me, right now, in this present moment.

We have in fact done the very thing with Yeshua's teachings that he cautioned us *not* to. We took the intimate, direct realization of Light within our very being and buried it beneath theological bushel baskets of ideological concepts. We have cut the direct experience of truth away from his teachings and choked out the very essence of what he urged us to maintain as the center point of our lives. We have become obsessed with the "Jesus finger" pointing at the moon, rather than awakening the direct experience of *the moon as us.* We have cultivated eyes that do not see and ears that do not hear – treasures in *mamoona*, an ancient Aramaic word that means *materiality,* not simply "money".

Let's go one step further and bring the point of the feminine nature of the Aramaic word *milta – "The Word"* – home. Your perception of these words that you are observing on this page are *feminine.* These actual, manifest, written words themselves are *masculine.* Are you picking up what I am telling you right now? *The "Word" is NOT a word on a page!* In fact, if you had implied in the first century that words written by the hand of a human were "the Word of God", except for maybe the earliest scrolls of the *Torah*, you would have been committing what in ancient times was called *goodapah*, which means *blasphemy.* The ancient near-Eastern meaning of blasphemy means "*to cut away or remove something from its true source or sustenance*".

In light of the feminine understanding of "the Word", it is not the masculine word on the page, but rather our feminine *perception* of that masculine manifestation. It is also not about the masculine words that we speak but rather about our feminine perception *as we speak*. The audible *mela*, or words that I speak are *masculine*, whereas mine and your perceptions of those sounds are *feminine.* In is not about the thing itself, it is about our choice of perception *of and as* "it". Are you understanding me yet?

Let's look across at the Greek to add even more nuance to this discussion. The original Koine Greek word for "the Word" – *logos* – is also not simply a word on a page. The Koine Greek word for "a word on a page", much like the Aramaic *mela*, was the word *lexis*, which was derived from the much older Proto-Indo-Eurpoean term *lego*, which meant a "spoken" or "written" word. When we mistake "the Word of God" as being a person, place or thing, we commit a blasphemy. We cut its true, intimate realization – within each and every one of us – off from its true source. I am right here and right now, at this exact point in human history, to help us let go of our ideological concepts *about* the deepest spiritual philosophies of the ages so that we can ultimately, on a cultural level, come into the direct realization of these eternal principles as the very essence of Life Itself – within, through and *as* us!

I have been very clear to the audiences in my speaking and sharing how I do not feel that I am here for those locked within the mass beliefs of generations who are set in their ways of what they are sure the "Jesus teachings" or the great philosophies of the world are all about. In contrast, I am here for the younger, or should I say *open generations of the future.* I am here to let the "powers that be" in this world know that those young ones who are birthing into this dimension will not tolerate the racist, homophobic, borderline psychopathic western Christian filth that has been done "in the name of Jesus". The same should hold forth for true Judaism and true Islam as well as all religions.

These fresh souls will not play our egomaniacal farce of mangling the greatest spiritual philosophies of the ages to feed the beast of our current political, religious and economic personas masquerading as "the only answer to humanity's ills". These young ones know that it was those who have come before them who have poisoned the rivers and streams of our mother earth and turned the air that we breathe into literal gas chambers. I am here for them, and for any and all souls of any age, gender, ethnicity or orientation who are willing to be open to birthing a much more authentic truth from within. I live by the words of Mahatma Gandhi "*The best way to find yourself is to lose yourself in the service of others.*"

I am here to tell those who wear these vulgar masks of ideological religion that we will play your game no longer. We are not here to judge our neighbor and cast ourselves as the "right" party in a war projected out in the world from our own unacknowledged inner demons. I am here to tell you that if any among us are not willing to love one another from the ground of our true being, then it is time for you to *step aside and sit down.* We are here to love, not to hate. We are here to live these deepest of eternal truths, not to fight over their "literal" (*i.e.* ideological) translation.

It is time for us to stop heaping useless information onto the souls of our young ones in the mad pursuit to indoctrinate and program them as fuel for the modern machine. It is time for our educational and theological systems to immediately stop the piling on of erroneous historical "facts" and modern "skillsets" and to instead begin to honor the true, essential nature of Light within each and every unique soul who incarnates on this planet.

In essence, each and every one of us are here to help humanity and life itself, in the words of civil rights leader Howard Thurman *"to come alive, because what the world needs now is people who have come alive"*. Now. The "Word of God" does not live on a page. The word of God is US, but only when we are awake enough to consciously live and be the very essence of our true, eternal nature in this present moment. *Now.*

"The misunderstanding [of philosophy] consists typically in misinterpreting mythological symbols as though they were references to historical facts.

In the Christian tradition, there is a very decisive problem in distinguishing between the sense of the word "Christ" and the sense of the word "Jesus". Jesus refers to an historical character. Christ is a reference to an eternal principle – the "Son of God" – the second person of the blessed trinity, which is before and after all the ages and is *not* historical"

JOSEPH CAMPBELL
"Misunderstood Philosophy"
[Lecture l.4.1]

Chapter 8

The *Miltha* Becomes Flesh

One August evening in 2009, I was walking down the hallway of my home past my then eight-year-old son Mikey's bedroom after breaking up a fight in the kitchen between him and his ten-year-old sister Lucynda. As I walked down the hall, I heard the sound "*ahhhhhwoooooon*" emanating from the narrow opening of Mikey's door. I stood quietly for a few moments, intrigued with what I was hearing. As I gently pushed the door open, I was greeted with a scene that I will remember for a lifetime and beyond. Mikey was sitting in the lotus position on the top bunk of his bed with the crown of his head just below the ceiling as he mindfully toned *"ahhhhhhwoooooon"*.

I stood there for a few moments before Mikey opened his eyes, flashed a bright, toothy smile and said *"I'm doing the abwoon daddy! It makes me feel better!"* Thrilled, though not wanting to interrupt him, I smiled and turned to leave and close the door behind me as a lump formed around my *vishuddhi* or throat chakra, while I reflected on this beautiful experience with my son. *Chakra* is a Sanskrit word meaning "spinning wheel," "cycle" or "circle" and refers to the energy points or nodes within the subtle energy body just in front of the spine where the *nadis* or "energy channels" meet. I feel my throat chakra expanding right now!

I returned to this experiment in my mind several years later when Mikey participated in a toning circle that I was facilitating in late 2013, when he was twelve years old. Mikey told me that how he felt while toning *abwoon* was one of the most amazing feelings he has ever had in his life. He also loved how it feels as it *"kind of echoes in my body"* after the actual toning is complete. Once again, here came a lump in my throat chakra. Wow.

Toning with children is one of the most enjoyable and rewarding aspects of all of my "work" in this world. They do not need, or often even want to know what the words *mean* before they tone them, they just want to get right to *feeling* them. We can learn so much from this, but only if we are not already too full of what we already "know" to be "the truth" about what the words "mean". Stay tuned for more about toning with children in this book, as well as in future books.

When I stepped into Mikey's bedroom that day, I immediately recognized the similarities with Robert Guillaume's character named Rafiki in *The Lion King* movie. The baboon Rafiki would sit and meditate in the lotus position atop a pile of earth, rock and roots near his favorite baobab tree, finger tips joined together and pointing skyward toward the heavens like a yogic master. When the princely lion Simba began to lose his way and "forget who he was", Rafiki shows up to not so gently remind him of his forgotten and mostly unrealized ground-root of his being, aka, his "father" Mufasa. *Simba* and *Rafiki* are Swahili words that mean *"lion"* and *"friend"* respectively. *Mufasa* is a Manazoto word meaning *"king"*.

Simba, unable to recognize "who I Am", is led by Rafiki down through a loud, confusing, chaotic wilderness beyond the flatland plains that Simba is much more familiar with into a dark, shadowy wooded area. As they arrive, Simba is panting heavily, his heart pounding in his chest. After they get through the intense cacophony of the jungle, Rafiki abruptly halts and yells *"Stop!"* He then pauses, turns back to Simba and says *"Shhhhhh!"* before taking a few more steps down to the edge of a cove, where he pulls some reeds to the side and whispers *"Look down there!"*, pointing toward the still pool below them.

What does Simba see as he steps forward and looks down onto the face of the deep waters? He sees *his own reflection.* Perplexed, Simba declares that what he sees is not his father, but *"just my reflection."* Rafiki advises Simba to look harder and says *"He lives IN you!"* Just then, Simba hears the echoing voice of his father, Mufasa, as he gazes skyward toward the great cosmic expanse out into space. Mufasa advises Simba to *"remember who you are"* and to take his place in the circle of life. Mufasa begins to fade back into the cosmos as he continues to repeat *"Remember who you are!" "Remember," "Remember."*

As Mufasa begins to recede from Simba's awareness, he panics and pleads for his father not to leave, still unaware of the eternal lesson he has just been given, that he in truth *IS* his father, appearing as a unique reflection within an eternal circle of life. Now, take one deep, cleansing breath before reading the following quote from St. Francis of Assisi:

"What you are looking for is what is looking".

The "father" that Simba is looking for lives *inside* of him or, much more accurately, his father continues to live *AS* him! The love, peace, Presence, creativity, fulfillment, purpose that you seek is in fact the very Presence-Energy which is seeking and seeing *through* you. It is your highest awareness, when you allow yourself to take a step back and observe the reflection that you see in your ego-mirror, as simply that – *a reflection.*

Paramahansa Yogananda called this reflection the *"pseudo soul".* The key is in the realization that what we are observing as an apparent "reflection" is in truth not separate in any way whatsoever from what is looking "at" it. And, of course the reflection is not what is "real", as it is simply a *reflection.* If we do not come into the direct realization of this eternal truth, then we will never, ever be able to "see" the Yeshua teachings in the fullness of their Light. We will simply obsess about the reflection of these teachings as they filter through our ideologies and religious belief systems *about* them.

We become so intensely focused on the "finger pointing at the moon" rather awakening into the direct, conscious realization that *we are the moon itself.* We are in the moon, and the moon is within us and, ultimately, there is no "moon", and there is no "us". The Greek word *angelos*, translated as *angel* means "messenger". Angelos is the source of the word *angle.* Each and every one of us are an apparently unique messenger – we are the angles of the eternal light as it projects and prismatically refracts into this realm of manifestation.

Even the slightest, subtlest nuance in translation can have a dramatic influence on our understanding of what that original teaching could possibly mean. I am quite happy to be viewed as a thorn in the side of many translators and scholars who choose to simply sit down and rest in the apparent safety of their theologies and belief systems. I resisted this facet of my life early on in my studies – back then I wanted to be "accepted". However, I refused to add labels before or after my name or to eat the force-fed conditioning that any theological or religious studies institution would program me with.

This made it much more difficult for many years in my work, yet now, in this very moment, I am much more authentically Dale Allen Hoffman. I think for myself, though definitely assisted by the immense research of those before and around me. And yes, that most definitely includes the experts. My work could never reach its true depth without their immense work and attention to detail. I am able to stand openly with this truth while also acknowledging the egomaniacal thrashing I have received over the years for not being a heavily accredited and accepted "real" scholar.

I read and study much of the materials and research of those coming from a place of fear and hostility who often feel a need to attack my life's work for being far too "experiential", which is most definitely not encouraged in the field. I recognize the brilliance of the study and research involved in scholarly work because I have done much of that research myself. In the end, however, the rubber must ultimately "meet the road". The truth is that if your translation does not reveal how to *live* what you are expounding as the "correct" translation, then you are in error. Period. Again, *what you are looking for is what is looking!*

I have said for years that if a translator simply makes one choice in the translation of a word or phrase with the intention of keeping it within his or her ideology or religious dogma, then they have failed at their job. My role is not to tell you *how* or *what* to think or believe. My job is to give you all of the fullest potentiality of possible nuance of what a word or phrase *could* mean and then allow you to find the jewel within that philosophy in the beating of your own heart. If, in my translation work, there is still a theologically confined word on the page such as "faith", "grace", "prayer", "glory", "the Word", or whatever that dogmatic term may be, then I have failed you, and I have failed myself.

If I am living up to the task presented to me, then I must also assist you in the unveiling of all of the deepest possible nuances of what that word or phrase could have meant in Yeshua's perspective. Remember what I wrote earlier in this book, if we dumb down the message to fit within only what the common, every contemporary person of Yeshua would have comprehended, then we have literally once again murdered the avatar as well as their wisdom. We choke out all of the possibility of what these teachings could have been seeking to communicate and we turn these eternal insights into nothing more than the popular, mainstream outlook of the common, everyday face in the crowd. *We must wake up right now, in this present moment!*

To move deeper into an intimate relationship with the greatest possible meanings inherent within the Gospel of John 1:14 King James Bible phrase "*the Word became flesh and dwelt amongst us*", let's breathe our way into the nuances of that verse. We will begin with the 1611 King James Version:

> "*And the Word was made flesh, and dwelt among vs (& we beheld his glory, the glory as of the onely begotten of the Father) full of grace and trueth.*"

This verse is a perfect example of the challenges that lie in offering forth a high-fidelity, less-filtered translation of Yeshua's ancient words that is not bound in the heavy religious theological dogma of words like *glory*, *grace* and *only begotten*. Not one of these terms existed in the first century because the English language itself did not even exist. While some of these words do have roots in older languages, our modern theological perspectives of Yeshua's ancient teachings must be let go of. If we cling to words like glory and grace without seeking to look beneath those common words to reveal what they actually *mean*, then we are exemplifying the very thing that chokes us off from any possibility of the direct realization of how to live the direct experience of these truths through the intimate fiber of our own spiritual lives.

Though these words from the Gospel of John are not attributed to Yeshua himself, they are incredibly rewarding in their depth of insight nonetheless. Since we have already spent quite a bit of time on the rich Aramaic term *milta*, let me unpack a few of the other central word meanings in this Aramaic verse, starting with the first sentence:

ܘܡܠܬܐ ܒܣܪܐ ܗܘܐ ܘܐܓܢ ܒܢ

omilta besrah haoeh oagen ban

And the *milta* is/becomes (*haoeh*) the flesh (*besrah*)
and lives (*oagen*) with, within, through, as and amongst us (*ban*)

Besrah is a word that literally means *flesh* and *haoeh* means "*turn*", "*be*", "*was*", "*is*" or "*become*". So, the traditional "*Word became flesh*" line is pretty accurate, other than the fact that we have mangled the translation of *milta* into simply "the Word". But there is much more going on here for eyes that see. Not only does the *milta* become flesh, but the *milta IS the flesh!* If you would like to breathe in a much wider comprehension of what this phrase embodies, go back to the previous chapter and re-read the list of example words offered for *milta.*

Of course, my focus in that section was that the *milta* – "the Word" is in no way separate from its ultimate process of manifesting as what is "obvious". There is no ancient Aramaic word for "effect" because we are speaking of one singular continuum or process, not two apparently different "parts" of one puzzle! The Light of the One is only fragmented and compartmentalized through our choice of thought, and not in its Absolute Truth *AS* us! When it is written earlier in the Gospel of John that "*nothing existed but through his hands*", that is not saying that a human-projected, anthropomorphized "God" built this physical world "with his hands", though I can't not chuckle out loud at the thought of that one.

The word translated in that verse as "hand" is *aydeh*, which means literally "*hand*", "*an extension of itself*", or "*as obvious as one's own hand*". It is also a word used for "*near*", "*obvious*" or "*through*" and points toward something extending or projecting itself into or through something that appears to be separate, yet is in fact "*obvious as an extension of itself*". The word *aydeh* was also used as one of the words for "neighbor", which means not only "*near in physical proximity*" so much as "*near in thought or mind*". In other words, the *milta* manifests into, through and *AS* itself – *AS US!*

Ban – the final word of the "*was made flesh and dwelt among us*" phrase – is almost always translated as simply "*amongst us*" or "*in our midst*", though stopping with that definition not only does our own inherent divinity a disservice, it also implies that "the Word" is somehow only *outside* of us, of which the Aramaic text is saying the exact *opposite* of! *Ban* means "*in*", "*into*", "*within*", "*in the midst of*" and "*through*". The prefix letter *beyt* in fact meant all of these things alone by itself. In other words, "the Word of God" did not simply become flesh and live amongst us, but rather, the "Word of God" becomes flesh and lives within, through and *AS* us! Don't you think that it may be just a tad important for the modern world to know this?

The *beyt* or "b" sound was often tagged onto the beginning of an ancient Aramaic word to connote the meanings of "*into*", "*inside of*", "*through*", or "*in the midst of*". Archdeacon *Sadook diMar Shimun* and Khabouris Codex Foundation scholars noted that the *beyt* or "b" prefix letter and the *lamed* or "l" prefix letter, were in truth distinctly separate and quite different from each other in meaning two millennia ago, though modern Syriac Aramaic has come to use the two interchangeably. The foundation scholars were not quite clear on when the mish-mash of these two different prefixes happened, though we now know that it did in fact occur. In contrast to the ancient "b" prefix, the "l" sound meant "*on*", "*toward*", "*at*" or "*against*". The "l" prefix pointed toward an interchange or relationship between two or more distinct persons, places or things while the "b" prefix was referring to a process within, through or *as* something.

One phrase that reflects the distinct quality, and subsequent mistranslations of this *beyt* prefix is John 20:22. This phrase is translated in the 1611 King James Bible as:

> "*And when he had said this, hee breathed on them, and saith vnto them, Receiue ye the holy Ghost.*"

This is another one of those phrases that elicits a chuckle from me and not only because of the peculiar capitalization of the word "Ghost" without capitalizing "holy" as well. Even using the word "ghost" is comical enough! Translating the ancient Aramaic *Rookha d'Koodsha* as "holy Ghost" is absolutely hilarious! I can even picture a ghostly apparition following us around, hiding around darkened corners and trying to "forgive our sins" exclaiming "Boo!" every time we do "a bad thing". *Bless their hearts!*

Rookha d'Koodsha is another one of those gorgeously experiential ancient Aramaic terms that is generally left untranslated. *Rookha d'Koodsha* is "*a feminine, un-created, yet creative eternal force of Alaha which undoes the errors in our ways of thinking and being as she teaches and recalibrates us back to Absolute Truth*". *Rookha d'Koodsha* is a feminine force within each and every one of us which is activated by our own conscious breath.

The Aramaic phrase translated as "*breathed on them*" is *npakh b'houn. Npakh* is derived from the Aramaic word *naphsha*, also usually left untranslated. *Naphsha*, most often translated as simply "*self*", is an Aramaic word that is usually laid next to the Greek *psyche*, most often translated as "*soul*", though the Aramaic *naphsha* is much more accurately translated literally as "*Breath of Life Itself*". As I just mentioned though, this definition can just barely scratch the surface of the ever-deepening layers that *naphsha* embodies, so it is often left untranslated.

The *ban* word is what is categorically translated as "*on them*", "*toward them*", or "*at them*", which of course erroneously implies only Yeshua himself as having the "*power of the Holy Spirit*" within himself and somehow needing to dole this power out to other, much less fortunate people around him. The theological ideology and belief system of Yeshua as a God-ordained "power person" will literally constrict any possibility of seeing this phrase with open eyes and an open heart.

The word "*them*" comes from the *oun* sound at the end of the word *b'houn*. *Houn* or *hoon* translates literally as "*them*", or "*all of you*". Now, remembering that the "b" and "l" prefixes have since become interchangeable in modern Syriac Aramaic, if we were to actually look at this ancient phrase in its 1st century context, "*on them*" would have to be written down as *l'houn*, as in "*he breathed ON them*". However, the Aramaic text actually reads *b'houn*, with the sole meanings of "*with them*", "*within them*", "*through them*" or "*in their midst*". Do you think that changes the meaning of that phrase? Does it ever! "*He breathed with them and said 'Receive rookha d'koodsha – the all-embracing eternal, feminine force of Absolute Truth.*" And of course, "*she*", as *rookha d'koodsha* was affectionately known in the first century, is activated by our own conscious breath, because *she IS the breath of our life*! Again, "*what you are looking for is what is looking*".

I will be more thoroughly unpacking this entire verse in a future book, though for now my focus is on that first line. So, let me conclude this chapter with my translation of the experiential breadth of this verse:

ܘܡܠܬܐ ܒܣܪܐ ܗܘܐ ܘܐܓܢ ܒܢ

omiltha besrah haoeh oagen ban

And the miltha is *(haoeh)* the flesh (*besrah*)

and lives (*oagen*) within, through, as and amongst us (*ban*)

ܘܚܙܝܢ ܫܘܒܚܗ ܫܘܒܚܐ ܐܝܟ ܕܝܚܝܕܝܐ

okhazeyn shoobkheh shoobkhah ahyk d'yikhidaya

And we realize the shimmering essence of true life (*shoobkheh*)

as the absolute radiance (*shoobkhah*)

of the non-dual human who is One with the All (*yikhidaya*)

ܕܡܢ ܐܒܐ ܕܡܠܐ ܛܝܒܘܬܐ ܘܩܘܫܬܐ

d'man abba damlea tayboota okooshta

and who is the ripe fruit of the absolute source (*abba*)
who is filled with the essence of (*damlea*) the ripe Presence (*tayboota*)
of absolute Truth (*okooshta*)

"He who esteems himself highly
on account of his knowledge
is like a corpse lying on the wayside:
the traveler turns his head away in disgust,
and walks quickly by"

RABBAI AKIVA BEN JOSEPH

CHAPTER 9

AWAKENED LIVING FROM THE ROOTED CENTER

As I mentioned earlier, when we mistake any object, be it any words on any page, or any person, as being "*the Word of God*", we do the very thing that Yeshua cautioned us *not* to do – we look at something that appears to be outside of our whole, undivided eternal Truth as the source of Being Itself. Truth is the very consciousness that is observing those words *through* us. "*The Law*" that Yeshua spoke of is not an ordinance or a fence for us to stay within the boundaries of. The true "*Law*" and the "*Word of God*" is the very essence that lives consciously *through* us when all boundaries of man-made religion, morals, ordinance and regulation are in fact *torn down!*

It was this outward worship of the letter of man's "God-given" ordinances, mistakenly labeled as law that is the very thing that Yeshua was exposing and brining out into our conscious awareness. This fragmented, outward focusing state of unconsciousness is only possible when we are relating with life from the shadowed viewpoint of our *eidolon*, which is the Greek word for *ego*. This eidolon, or *pseudo-soul* as Paramahansa Yogananada called it, is built upon a shaky base of fear – *false evidence appearing real.*

The words on the page are not "*The Word*", nor is our fallible, individualized religion-based human facsimile of it. It is the direct transmission of consciousness *through* us that is the true "*Word of God*".

The Christian Holy Bible is a book, an avenue, a finger pointing at the moon, a path. Yet, *the map is not the terrain.* No map is perfect, whole or complete. There is always more detail, nuance and perspective that can be revealed and added to the topography as far as we are able to recognize and comprehend it. Yet *the map is also not the destination.* The destination is in the direct experience *itself.* The true "Word of God" – *the Milta – is Life Itself!*

I live deep within the Appalachian Mountains of Western North Carolina. When viewed on a flat map, our mountain roads look fairly straight with maybe a curve here and a curve there. However, for one who is not skilled in driving on mountain roads, the experience may begin as a harsh reality check. Regardless of how seemingly straight a road may appear on a flat map, the experience of actually driving on these roads can be very challenging. They go up, they go down, hairpin turns followed by acute switchbacks and drops of several hundred or even a thousand feet, often with no road shoulder in sight. Again, *the map is not the terrain.*

My childhood experiences of sensing and feeling the much deeper, experiential qualities of the words on the page did not at the time feel like a revelation. At the time, it actually felt like I just didn't get it. I was the odd man out. Everyone else – pastors, teachers, and fellow students – all seemed to be in agreement on the definition of those words, yet not one of them seemed to *understand how those teachings are meant to be lived.*

I somehow sensed at that young age that just because I think that I understand a collection of definitions in my head does not in any way whatsoever mean that I will automatically *feel* the direct realization of those meanings, no matter how well defined, in my heart. I have taken a lot of flak for this view over the years from countless biblical scholars who enjoy entertaining themselves by mocking the living heart of my life's work as well as that of Neil Douglas-Klotz, Rocco Errico, Dr. Michael Ryce and George Lamsa, among others.

I have received hate mail, death threats, and I am occasionally mocked in message boards and chat rooms on scholarly web sites. I have even had hacking attempts on my social media accounts by religious zealots. After years of taking these attacks personally, I can now speak of these situations with a huge smile of gratitude on my face because I have actualized the truth that if anyone is able affront these kinds of attacks on *anyone*, then they have absolutely no clue what the "Jesus teachings" which they memorize, espouse and use as weapons actually *mean* anyway. If they did, then the fruits of their life would reveal that they are in fact *living it*. Again, these emotions of judgment, fear and hostility can only come from the *ego*, and never from the True Self.

Clearly, I am not meant to fit into a box. I am not here to buy into excessive conditioning. I am here to be *open*. Of course, not all conditioning is a bad thing. Knowing when not to walk out onto a busy street or why drinking poison is not recommended are both useful bits of information. I feel that I am here to allow myself to see these teachings as I did at the age of seven – *from my heart*.

Do I study? Absolutely! I read scholarly journals, I pore through the textbooks and I sit beside native near Eastern Syriac Aramaic souls and ask them about their heritage. But I do not have a horse in the race. *I am here to be open*. I am very clear that I would not be able to realize much of the depth of my work without the meticulous, scientific language studies and research of the giants whose shoulders I often stand upon. I have always been very vocal in saying that I need them on some level. However, I am quite often reminded and told that I am not a "real" scholar. And to that end, I feel a great heritage of honor. I just want to be *real*.

In the years after my first experiences with Dr. Michael Ryce, I devoured everything that I could on ancient languages, specifically Aramaic, Greek, Hebrew and Coptic, though also going much further back to Akkadian, Phoenician and quite a few indigenous languages. I studied everything I could get my hands on. I was especially "lit up" by the work of the late *Rev. Sadook de Mar Shimun*, former Archdeacon of the Assyrian Church of the East. I was fascinated with how he was able to distill the ancient Aramaic nuance of the direct, experiential meanings of Yeshua's teachings down to its bare essentials without letting modern viewpoints of theology get in the way of the fidelity of first century meaning.

The bulk of the mainstream materials available about the Aramaic in the mid 1990's often left me feeling so incredibly unfulfilled due to their resistance of letting go of the predominant fences of theology and an inability to just "say it like it is". I realized that theology, though quite valuable in its place, can also be an effective way to divert attention away from a deep lack of true realization of the inner, experiential meanings of the teachings beyond the words on the page. It can be a very effective subterfuge to cover up the reality of spiritual immaturity.

While one may be able to endlessly explain the theological or linguistic reasons why the words on the page are this way or that way, if we are to realize these eternal principles, then we must be willing to bring these teachings into the deeper spaces of the heart. If we allow the predominant, widely-accepted thought patterns and theological belief systems of academia and conventionally lauded scholarship to remain bulletproof and unchecked, then we will literally choke out the very last kernel of the living essence of the true "*Word of God*", right down to its final gasp for air.

In other words, I can write a 5,000 page book about the taste of chocolate. My "correct" and well-researched book can have a multitude of words and phrases with which I can thoroughly explain the amazing taste of chocolate, its character profile nuances and embodied characteristics, *ad nauseum*. But can these definitions, seemingly in depth words and commentary about the taste of chocolate, no matter how detailed and accurate, ever take the place of the actual, direct experience of tasting chocolate? *Can it?* The original Gnostic Yeshua teachings were about the direct, intimate experience of *tasting the sacred*, not the description *about* the experience. He showed us how to *live it*. Somewhere on the road, we seemed to forget this. And then some.

Also, if we allow our understanding of the ancient Aramaic teachings attributed to Jesus to simply rest upon what a common, everyday first century Judean resident's colloquial understanding of the words may have been, then we will again remain cut off from the direct *experiences* which his teachings were directing us into. As I mentioned earlier, we can so easily become obsessed with the "Jesus finger" rather than actualizing the direct realization of what he was *pointing at!* If we are to grow in our experience and understanding what the words mean within the depth of our heart and being, then we must continue to reveal the absolute fullest potentiality inherent within their possibilities of meaning. If we do come do this, then the transformational depth of what was written down will remain locked up in our well-intentioned, though often misguided intellectual boxes.

A common self-imposed bias that I often hear is *"Yeah, but weren't they all just illiterate, backwater yokels back then?"* And therein lies another often tragic impediment to the personal integration of a great teaching or philosophy from the inside out. As I mentioned earlier, if we dumb down the Yeshua teachings by restraining their immensity down to the level of the common man's first century understanding of them – or of a modern 21st century scholar's widely accepted definition of it – rather than treating these cosmic philosophies as we would those of any true avatar, then we have in essence, once again, "killed the messenger". When the common, colloquial, everyday meanings of an eternal philosophy become more important than awakening the widest possible breadth of meaning embedded within it, then we shall surely die along with that bias. Again, *it is time for us to "grow up" spiritually, take a few steps back, and to allow "the Jesus story" to grow up as well.*

This excerpt from the Khabouris Codex Institute's "Enlightenment" publication illustrates my concern succinctly:

"A dialog between Archdeacon di Mar Shimun and other Foundation Scholars, is a case in point: Each scholar made his renderings of the Khabouris independently, and then all the renderings were tested and harmonized by all the scholars in concert. At one point in the process, there was disagreement between Archdeacon di Mar Shimun and some of the other scholars regarding the rendering of the word normally translated as "neighbor". The other scholars contended that the word meant: "only those in close physical proximity", similar to our normal usage today. Archdeacon di Mar Shimun, however, knew that this definition was artificially limited and that the word 'neighbor' actually meant more to the ancient Aramaic speaking people. Specifically, "anyone you are aware of (including self)."

After much correspondence and debate, Archdeacon explained the reason for the discrepancy: *"I know what the problem is; the others are using those new dictionaries - you know; the ones from the 6th century – the ones changed by the Moslem Invaders. We must be using the definitions from the 1st century to be true to the understanding of the Ancients."*

Faith is not a religion or a system of beliefs, but rather the pure, rooted direct experience of *being consciously lived as Life Itself.* In His teaching, the faith that Yeshua spoke of is not simply a collection of beliefs and memorized ideological programming. One of the questions that I often get asked is *"What is your faith?"* My response is always deeply heartfelt: *"What does faith mean to you?"* Faith means very different things to different people. Our modern thought process about the ancient Aramaic word for faith – *hayyemanoota* – has virtually vanished, buried under the theological hay pile of two thousand years of misunderstanding and a strong lack of recalibration to the original first-century meaning of this experiential term that is one of the very core roots of Yeshua's teachings.

Hayyemanoota is a combination of several Aramaic root sounds which, when recalibrated and brought back together, reaffirm the very central essence of what the original teachings were communicating to those with "eyes that see and ears that hear". Semitic languages, once understood as "building block" or "puzzle" tone poems, can be fairly simple to comprehend on deeper levels, beyond the common, every day, widely acknowledged meanings of these ancient words from our modern perspective. Reading the words of Yeshua in ancient Aramaic reveals a deep experience of language full of infinitely layered meanings, contextual nuance, idioms, syntax and gorgeously intriguing Aramaic word play and poeticism that is often completely unseen in the Koine Greek or any subsequent translation of any kind.

The Aramaic language is built upon very clearly defined, simple root sounds. If one has a strong enough understanding of each of the ancient root sound meanings of an Aramaic word, we can often define the word by recombining the meanings of those root sounds into one cohesive whole. This is something that Archdeacon Shimun was an absolute master at in his translation work with the Aramaic Khabouris manuscript, and also something that has been virtually swept aside by most modern Aramaic language dogmatists in favor of much more conceptual, strictly theological interpretations. The Khabouris manuscript is an 11th century copy of a 2nd century Syriac Aramaic New Testament text.

I am incredibly enthused by the fresh wave of budding, open hearts within *esotericism* who are so beautifully self-effacing and willing to let go of the more widely-accepted colloquial or theologically accepted meanings. These brave souls are walking their talk and remaining open enough to be able to grasp the gorgeous tree of life which is concealed just below the surface of the common, everyday meanings.

The future looks bright for us to enter into a deeper truth and light a more authentic path for what I have for many years been calling *The Generation of Light*. They are birthing into this dimension with an innate brilliance and inner sense of intelligence that humanity has never seen before. We have in fact entered into the "Seventh Generation" that the Lakota spoke of in the second half of the 19th century and continue to honor today for our future generations. *We are the one that we have been waiting for!*

Before looking deeper into the word "faith", let's look at the "puzzle sounds" of a word to understand this a bit better. As an example, the Aramaic word *sney* means *hate* or *malice*. By itself, *sney* is simply a word. If I add the *ta* suffix at the end, then we now have the word *sneyta*. The *ta* is a feminine gendered sound which means *"a hateful attitude, perception, or state of being."* So *sney* is the word "*hate*" and *sneyta* is a "*hateful perception or state of being*".

From a more clearly defined psychological perspective, this description of the ancient Aramaic *ta* sound, again from the Khabouris Codex Institute's "Enlightenment" publication:

"The suffix "-ta" indicates the root concept is a present mind set, or attitude, a force on the mind exercising a control function over what can be perceived, what can be stored in or recalled from memory and what can be used in judgment formation.

If I add the *oo* sound into the middle to create the word *sneyoota*, it now becomes *hateful action*. The letter *waw* – the *oo* sound – is a bit like the *ing* suffix in English, it connotes action or behavior, as in from *walk*, to *walking*. So, broken down, *sney–oo–ta* or *sneyoota*, is a "*hateful perception is being acted out*". Let's open this up with one more quote from the Aramaic Khabouris Codex Institute:

"The use and meaning of these suffixes confront us with the question of what is represented by the root word standing alone when it is without the "-ta" or the "-oota" suffix, when it is not an active mind set or attitude nor active behavior and judgment. Thus *sneyoota* is active malicious, vicious behavior and judgment, *sneyta* is the attitude or mind set productive of malicious, vicious behavior and judgment. But what is designated by *sney*? Apparently the root word to which a *ta* or *oota* can be appended represents a stored mental capacity, a latent, finite entity of mind, available yet inactive, a mind structure or formation developed, inherited, planted or otherwise acquired and readily available for activity."

It is quite a bit like a puzzle, isn't it? Now let's look at "*faith*" – *hayyemanoota*. The word *hayyemanoota* is built upon four basic root sounds

– *hayye*, *iman*, *oo* and *ta*. Let's go in reverse, from the end of the word back to the beginning. As I have just explained, the *ta* sound points to a state of being, attitude or perception, which is *feminine*. Faith in the ancient Aramaic sense of the word is not a masculine noun, a "person", "place" or "thing", but rather *a perception, an attitude, a state of being or a direct "spiritual" experience*. If we add the *oo* sound into the word, *faith* now blossoms not only as a state of being but through our behavior and actions as well.

The primary root sound of the word *hayyemanoota* is the sound *iman*, which is still the word for "faith" in Arabic today. *Iman* is a sound that has been in the ancient Aramaic language as far back as around the 10th century bce. This sound can also be found in Hebrew, Coptic Egyptian and possibly in Akkadian as well. The *alef – mem – nun* consonant sequence is also the root of the ancient Aramaic word *Ahmeyn*, which we know more often in the west as *"Amen"*. The "a – m – n" letter root is derived from an ancient root sound meaning *"from the fertile, rooted earth center"*. I will offer much more insight into the Aramaic word *ahmeyn* in the final toning section of this book. For now, let's just keep it simple and say *"from the center"*.

The first sound in *hayyemanoota* is the sound *hayye*. *Hayye* is what Yeshua said he had *"come to give us abundantly"*. And what was that? *Life Itself!* Hayye is an incredibly rich word in Aramaic, meaning something closer to *"essential life energy"* at its root. *Hayye* can also mean *conscious*, as in *"awareness"*, as well as *strength*, *power* or *will*.

So we have four root sounds meaning "conscious life", "rooted center", "action" or "behavior" and "attitude" or "being". So the ancient Aramaic meaning of faith – *hayyemanoota* – is closer to *"consciously living from the rooted center of being."* In other words, one does not have faith in some *THING* – such as a religion, belief, ideology or concept – but rather that faith is the direct experience or state of being in which we are *consciously being lived by Life Itself*. If you are telling me that you "*have faith in*" some belief system or "*faith that something will happen*", then you are already reveling in some "*thing*" or end outcome outside of you, which is in truth a *lack* of faith! That is nothing more than belief or trust, and it most definitely is *NOT* faith. You are telling about something that you do not have, realize or possess, and that is the *opposite* of faith, regardless of your belief in any specific outcome, effect or end result.

We do not *have* faith in something – that is simply *belief*. Rather, we live consciously *AS* the faith of Life Itself – from the grounded, rooted center of all true Being. In the words of poet ee cummings, *"the root of the root and the bud of the bud."* Faith is not about what we "*believe in*", faith is who we are, at our deepest, most essential core, which is Life Itself. *Faith is who we are being and living AS!*

[Jesus said:] "Seek not the law in your scriptures, for the law is life, whereas the scripture is dead. I tell you truly, Moses received not his laws from God in writing, but through the living word. In everything that is life is the law written. You find it in the grass, in the tree, in the river, in the mountain, in the birds of heaven, in the fishes of the sea; but seek it chiefly in yourselves. For I tell you truly, all living things are nearer to God than the scripture, which is without life.

God wrote not the laws in the pages of books, but in your heart and in your spirit. They are in your breath, your blood, your bone; in your flesh, your bowels, your eyes, your ears, and in every little part of your body. They are present in the air, in the water, in the earth, in the plants, in the sunbeams, in the depths and in the heights.

They all speak to you that you may understand the tongue and the will of the living God."

THE ESSENE GOSPEL OF PEACE, BOOK ONE
[Translated from Aramaic by Edmond Bordeaux Szekely]

CHAPTER 10

AWAKENING *PARADISE*

I continue to cultivate my conscious recognition of the deeper meanings beyond the simple, colloquial and widely accepted definitions of the words on the page. It is only when I allow my understanding to ripen and mature that I can begin to awaken the process of inner knowing that unlocks greater capacities of my understanding of "*The Word*". Clearly, we need those common, surface meanings to begin our journey into realization. Actualization, however, requires much a much deeper, directly experienced relationship with the living, breathing core of these universal, eternal truths.

This deep spiritual and psychic ripening awakens us to our inherent divinity as an intimate, deeply personal, yet somehow completely holistic and impersonal realization of ourselves as the conscious channels of the infinite present in this apparent dimension of time and space. It is only in seeing beyond the obvious, masculine words on the page that we can in truth reawaken the direct, feminine essence of realization through our hearts and lives and graduate the earth-bound curriculum to finally leave the classroom and actually *live it!*

One very profound way of enriching our experiential relationship through a sacred text is awakened through a process of seeing deeper into the experiential meanings of the words that have been right here beneath our noses the entire time. As an example, each letter of the

Hebrew alphabet embodies four distinct levels, or what is called *pardes* of interpretation (*exegesis*) and layers of meaning. The Hebrew PRDS is an acronym which birthed the Persian root of what would ultimately become the English word *"Paradise"*. When one is able to, through revelation or inspiration, unlock the deeper "*secret*" or "*mystery*" meanings of a sacred text, we ultimately awaken paradise.

Pardes is a Hebrew word with Persian roots meaning "*orchard*" or "*garden*" and could today even be used as the word for what we call a nature preserve or park, i.e. *paradise.* As soon as *pardes* is let out of the box, this is the point where many literalists make a hasty exit from the room because many believe the less masculine, much less clearly defined feminine intangibles to be far too elusive and "not real enough" to warrant serious and "real" study. So be it, because that is exactly where we are going.

Let's look at the four distinct levels of *pardes* when opening the deeper, experiential meanings embedded within a sacred text.

PESHAT

The plain, simple, obvious or "surface" level meaning.

REMEZ

The allegorical "hints" or deeper meanings;
Beyond the simple, literal meanings.

DRASH

The comparative, or *midrashic* meanings, in which one seeks to reveal the common threads of meaning which run through the essential core of a word as it is used in different contexts.

SOD

The "secret" or hidden "mystery" meaning;
Experiential meaning unveiled through awakened revelation.

Let's take a deeper look into each of the four levels of *pardes*. The top *peshat* level of interpretation is where literalists and fundamentalists most often reside. This is also where the literal scholar hangs his hat as well, though some literalists may occasionally allow themselves to dip down into the top edge of *remez – the allegorical level –* as well. However, when a literalist does yield to any possibility of deeper meaning, they will often attach a caveat of disclaimer as well.

To remain at the *peshat* level requires that no interpretation remain open ended and all loose ends must be tied up in literality. This is what Yeshua referred to as seeds falling on *arid* or "*evil*" soil. The Aramaic word for evil is *bisha*, which means "*not fully fertile or ripe in this present moment.*" In other words, "*eyes that do not see and ears that do not hear*".

However, none of the three deeper levels of *pardes* could in truth exist without the *peshat* level of literality, whether we are aware of a literal meaning or not. *Peshat* is the ground level, the base. Though as we move deeper through the four levels of *pardes*, we are not building *up* from the base of *peshat*, but instead more accurately digging down *below* the base of this surface level meaning into the less clearly regimented, much more feminine and experiential aspects of meaning. Again, the literal level is absolutely essential. Yet, digging deeper toward the "*secret*" or "*experiential*" meanings is a matter of personal choice. How far do you choose to go?

The second *remez* level is the allegoric or symbolic meanings that even every day speakers may at least be aware of. In modern English, an example would be how someone saying, "*Wow, that's deep*", would not necessarily mean depth into the earth as in down into a hole, but rather something that is reaching far below a more common, surface level of understanding. This would apply whether it be physical or, in the case of *remez*, metaphorical. The *remez* level is where most late 19th and early 20th century metaphysical teachings reside, though they may at times also dip into the *drash* and even occasionally into the *sod* levels. Some of the more recent metaphysical teachings of the late 20th century into our modern day have been diving much deeper into the *drash* and *sod* levels. This is an exciting development in spiritual growth and comprehension beyond the abundant New Thought teachings of the early 1900s.

The third level of interpretation – *drash* – is sourced from the Hebrew word *darash*, which means to "*inquire*" or "*seek*". *Drash* is the comparative or *midrashic* meanings in which one would compare similar occurrences where a particular word appears in one or more texts, and to seek to reveal the common threads of meaning which runs through the essential core of this word when used in different contexts. This is usually accomplished by breaking a word down into its basic root sound meanings which combine and work together to create a word's overall meaning.

The *sod*, or "secret" level requires an openness to all levels of interpretation equally. It does not counteract or contradict any of the nuances of meaning within any of the other three levels of *pardes* but by its very nature seeks to reveal implicit harmony between all four layers inclusively as one unified whole. The hidden or "secret" meaning reveals its often subtle, much more feminine or experiential nuance through revelation or *gelyana*, which is an Aramaic word meaning "*to unveil*". This unveiling happens when one is *touv*, or wholly "*ripe*" and "*fertile*" in the present moment. This would again come back to Yeshua's metaphor of "*ripe*" or "*fertile*" (*touv*) and "*arid*", "*unripe*" or "evil" (*bisha*) soil. When we are fully present and open, she reveals herself through the fertile ripeness of our open heart. *Sod* is not about simply believing or knowing. *Sod is about realization and being.*

In many first century Semitic cultures, especially those of a more Gnostic or experiential nature, when a teaching or text was referred to as a "secret", it did not simply mean that a particular text was to be hidden away to prevent non-initiates from seeing its surreptitious contents, though this was definitely done at times. The secret meaning of a teaching, word or text was more often referring to a common language teaching, word or phrase that was right there on the page, often in full access to the public, right in front of our face. However, the true depth of its meaning remains concealed to the naked eye unless one has "*eyes to see and ears to hear*".

In his 1929 book "*Pagan Regeneration: A Study of Mystery Initiations in the Greco-Roman World*", Harold R. Willoughby relayed how the general mass of students were called *mystae*, meaning "*those with closed eyes*" until they went through their final grade of spiritual initiation, at which point they were called *epopteia*, meaning "*those who can see*". These "eyes closed" *mystae* were often very easily swayed and wowed by the "bells and whistles" of miracles, trance states and even psychotropic substances, most often to the negation of true actualization and realization. In the eagerness of their spiritual immaturity, they would often prefer to be "stoned on God" rather than do what was required to experience the eternal nectar of true Gnosis. This "*eyes that can see and ears that can hear*" insight was literally all over the pagan philosophies and mystery teachings at the time of Yeshua. In fact, this pagan philosophy is all over the teachings of Yeshua as well.

When looking at Semitic teachings, this "*eye-opening*" process can be fostered and stimulated through a study of the combined letter meanings of a word – literally, translating it letter by letter rather than simply as a complete word unto itself. Very few westerners realize that the Hebrew Torah was originally read not word for word or verse by verse, but rather *toned letter by letter*. The earliest texts of the Torah were actually more like a mathematical algorithm or string of characters, as in a universal constant such as *pi*, with no spaces or punctuation of any kind.

The essence or intent was to observe not only each character unto itself, but also through its inclusive relationship within the entire text itself. This would be much like ruminating on one single puzzle piece while also opening one's awareness to how this one piece fits holistically within the whole of the text itself. The Torah was not, and is not today simply spit out and spoken as much as it is toned or sung consciously in deep states of receptivity. It was hundreds of years *after* the writing of the original Torah texts before they were broken down into words and verses, final letter forms, phonetic markings and spaces between words.

In order to awaken the *sod* level of a teaching, one must first enter through what Yeshua referred to as trying to get a "*rope through the eye of a needle*". The word that Yeshua used for "*eye*" is *khrooreah*, which means "*opening*", "*portal*", "*freedom*", "*emancipation*", "*liberty*", "*opening*" or "*eye*". The word *khrooreah* literally means "*to free a slave*".

The Yeshua teachings also used the Aramaic word *tareah* several times to describe this wholly open and surrendered state of being. *Tareah* is most often translated as *"doorway"*, *"gate"*, *"doorkeeper"* or *"gatekeeper"*. *Tareah* would be much more accurately translated as *portal* – a doorway or entry point between two rooms or dimensions of awareness. The *sod* level is revealed only through states of deep meditation and contemplation, when one is empty and open, though not necessarily by conscious choice. This open emptiness can often come through an experience of immense challenge, confusion or profound loss. *Gelyana* develops and grows through the fertile, open portal when we finally let go.

Many of us have felt this feeling in meditation or moments of deep spiritual experience. It is what I call "*falling backward off a cliff with your eyes closed into an abyss of not knowing*". This moment does not always feel like roses and sunshine, but in truth often feels more like an overwhelming state of panic or loss of control. Yet this is exactly what is required. Your acute fear in these moments is simply the echoing resonance of your hidden past.

It is written in an abundance of rabbinic literature that first and second century *Rabbi Akiva ben Joseph* was the only of four men who entered into *pardes* and lived. Rabbai Akiva "*entered in peace and left in peace.*" The influence of Rabbi Akiva, who was instrumental in drawing up the canon of the Hebrew *Tanakh*, on esoteric, mystic and Kabbalistic Jewish philosophies cannot be understated. *Esoteric* is a word derived from the Greek *esoterikos*, meaning *"far within"*. Several accounts exist of Akiva's death and most of them speak of Akiva having been stripped naked and ultimately "*stripped of his skin*" at the hands of the Romans.

Rabbi Akiva's teachings were often focused on transcending the illusions of duality. The life blood of his work has long resonated for me because he so eloquently balanced his goal of continually stimulating the evolution of his own scholarly pursuits while never losing sight of the experiential core at the center of his spiritual path. Neither purely a scholar nor purely a mystic, he was able to stay open and awaken the sacred balance between the two. I can personally acknowledge that this is no small feat and requires continual vigilance, personal accountability, authenticity and openness.

Akiva's often heavily attacked and criticized teachings offered the recognition of cultivating the insight to realize that all apparent dualities are in truth unique qualities within one singular continuum or process of being – a *modus operandi*. As an example, when one comes into the realization that the inside does not exist separately from the outside, the positive from the negative, the light from the dark, the masculine from the feminine – we awaken into the conscious experience of paradise living *as* us through our very beingness. Meister Eckhart so brilliantly wrote that *"There is no being except in a mode of being"*.

Rabbi Akiva, though stripped of his physical clothes, was in truth not "naked" at all in the spiritual sense. In his book "Echoes of Eden: Sefer Bereishit Volume 4", Ari D. Kahn refers to Akiva having been wearing "*clothing of light*" and a "*garment of light and truth*". It is only when we let go, when we surrender what we "know" and rest back within the non-reflected emptiness, that we realize our true oneness within the sacred. This is the realization of true *Gnosis*.

Much like the Sufi idea of the "inside like the outside" or the self-similar fractal nature of the *implicate order* and *explicate order* referred to by theoretical physicist David Bohm, Yeshua spoke of the "garment" in the Coptic Gospel of Thomas:

> "When you disrobe without being ashamed and take up your garments and place them under your feet like little children and tread on them, then [will you see] the Son of the Living One, and you will not be afraid"

Who is the "Son of the Living One?" *It is you!* It is the moment of your realization that your apparent reflection in the *ego-mirror* is in fact not separate from that which observing it. And yet, what you see in the mirror is not what is real, nor is what it is reflecting. Both are simply echoes. What is "real" is awareness. Again, *"what you are looking for is what is looking."* Incidentally, the three Aramaic words that can be translated as "skin" – *gelda, garbah* and *meshka* – can all also be translated as *"hide"*. *Garbah* is also a word for *bottle, jar* or *pitcher*, which may bring to mind Yeshua's teachings on how "new wine" should not be placed in "*old wineskins, lest they burst.*" The Aramaic word *man* means *vessel, garment, receptacle, implement* or *utensil.* The word translated as wineskin is *zakeah,* which also means *bag* or *container*. The primary Aramaic word for "garment" is *nakhta*, which also means *"to descend into a valley"*, very likely a reference to the psychic *"fall of man"*.

Arthur M. Young referenced this mythic "*fall of man*" in his book *The Reflexive Universe*, of our descent from light into matter.

> "Recent developments in physics, quantum physics in particular, when properly understood, provide confirmation for the ancient notion of a fall. We may now show that it is true, in fact, that a fall occurs, for the same process by which light first precipitates or condenses into matter – *losing a degree of freedom in exchange for permanence* – a descent from the freedom of light into the inertness of matter."

The much more feminine *sod* dimension cannot reveal herself until we wholly let go of any need to understand, comprehend or to *get it.* This experience can also unfold in moments of hitting rock bottom, when we can finally admit that we, our finite selves, do not "*know*". And so we release the reigns of control and finally let go of needing to intellectually comprehend. It is only after this letting go, the opening of the *tareah – portal*, that the true foundation of the deepest meanings can reveal themselves through the clarity of our open eyes and spacious heart.

I often refer to *gelyana* as the feminine revelation who quietly sneaks up behind you and gently wraps her arms around you as she opens up a depth of awareness that is beyond our normal waking states of comprehension. If you are a parent, imagine an experience where your young child does this very thing without notice. You are sitting and possibly feeling overwhelmed and your young one quietly comes up behind you, wraps her arms tightly around you, and begins to breathe, all without saying a single word. This is the power of *rookha d'koodsha*, or the "*the all-embracing feminine breath of God*", known in modern times as simply the "*holy ghost*" or "*holy spirit*".

Rookha d'koodhsa was often referred to in the first century as simply "*she*". She is the all-embracing feminine Breath of the One who undoes the effect in our erroneous ways of thinking and being. She cannot enter until we let go. When we do, she brings us deep into the mothering space of her womb, where we feel whole, complete, connected to the cosmic Source-Energy of Creativity Itself. Neil Douglas-Klotz calls this state of *being "The I Can of the cosmos."* In truth, there are no "secrets", only deepening layers of Self-realization. And rightly so.

"Since purpose is in the whole and not in the parts, the whole must be greater than the parts. How can we account for this? Because the whole *cannot function when divided*. It follows that function is that aspect of "cause" which is not in the parts and which science cannot deal with, because science deals with mass, length and time, which are parts. This leads to a basic cosmological postulate: *the parts are derived from the whole*, and not the whole from the parts. In other words, the whole exists *before* the parts."

ARTHUR M. YOUNG
From the book *The Reflexive Universe*
[Anodos Foundation]

CHAPTER 11

SURFING THE FRACTAL EDGE OF THE COSMIC EXPANSION

The first line of the Hebrew Torah can be translated at least 913 distinct ways from its original ancient Hebrew into either Greek or English. *"In the beginning God created the heavens and the earth"* is just one of those hundreds of ways. In fact, this first line of what Christians call the Old Testament, is one of the most fascinating as well as richly nuanced lines to untangle in all of the world's most beloved sacred literature.

As I mentioned in the previous chapter, most people do not realize that the beginning of the Hebrew Torah was not originally simply a story of words, verses and chapters, but in fact a string of characters, much like an algorithm or mathematical equation. Is was one long run-on string that was read not word for word and verse by verse but rather letter by letter. The segregation and breaking down of this ancient text into words with final markers, as well as verses, chapters and topical story lines, did not happen until hundreds of years later. This is *very* important!

I am very clear that if you are not reading a teaching, philosophy or religious precept in its original language, then much of its nuance of meaning, depth and richness immediately flies out the window. That is not to say that all translations are without value, but rather that it is quite essential to acknowledge that something must fall by the way side with each subsequent translation of a sacred text, regardless of the skill and/or consciousness of its translator. It is simply unavoidable.

What would ultimately become the first five books of the 1611 Holy Bible (aka, the "Authorized" King James Bible) in fact was not sourced entirely from the original Hebrew Pentateuch, the Five Hebraic Books of Moses from the Torah, but also from the *Septuagint*, a third through first century BCE translation of the original Hebrew Bible into the much more limited and sparse Koine Greek. *Septuaginta* is a word of Latin origin meaning "seventy", in reference to the number of scholars who worked over the course of almost two hundred years to complete this translation.

Though the KJV was partially drawn from some Hebrew and Aramaic texts, as well as from Daniel Bromberg's 1524 Hebrew Rabbinic Bible, much of the "Old Testament" which King James-raised western Christians have been raised on is quite far in context and meaning from the ancient Hebrew Torah that Yeshua – a first century near Eastern Semite – would have been raised on. The Christian Old Testament is in fact a surface level allegorical translation of something far deeper in its lush, multi-layered richness that often cannot even be comprehended in the Greek or Latin languages, let alone fully translated into any language outside of its original Hebrew.

From its first inception, the Hebrew Bible, in the words of its contemporary Jewish rabbis, could only be compared to *itself*. The legions of rabbis of the day were very publicly vocal in their admonishment of what they called "the greatest tragedy in the history of humanity" – the translation of the original Hebrew Torah into its Septuagint Greek copy.

If Yeshua were an actual first century Galilean Semitic Jew, as we have been told, he would have not in any way learned from the Greek Septuagint translations that we derive our modern Christian teachings from. To do so would have been sacrilege of the absolute highest order. He would have been a Torah-abiding Jew and would have been hearing and reading from ancient Hebrew Torah scrolls, not from metaphoric Greek renderings and re-translations.

Yeshua would have had to have a strong base of Hebrew to be Jewish, plus he would have been fluent in Aramaic, the *lingua franca* of the first century CE Galilean region. In Yeshua's time, Hebrew was regarded as the "sacred" language, to be spoken primarily in the Temple and at sacred gatherings, where Aramaic was the much more common, colloquial language of the day.

I have to laugh when I hear someone try to argue that Yeshua was in fact not an Aramaic speaker, but rather only a Hebrew speaker. Of course, if Yeshua was an actual man who walked the earth in that time and place, He would have spoken Hebrew, *He was Jewish!* But offering "proof" that He spoke Hebrew does not in any way prove that He did not speak Aramaic, it simply offers evidence that he spoke Hebrew. Of course He did! Again, *He was Jewish!*

We are going to spend a bit of time looking at a few of the nuances of the beginning of Genesis in its original Hebrew. The Hebrew letters (as with Aramaic) read from right to left. The reason for this was because, in the process of etching or carving words, the scribe's hand that held the carving device would not cover up and conceal the letter that they were working on. *Beresheet*, translated as *"In the Beginning"*, is in fact the Hebrew word ultimately translated into English as *Genesis.*

Beresheet

←בראשית←

It would never be possible to reveal the deeper meanings inherent within the Hebrew *beresheet* if we were lost in the surface *peshat* level translation as simply *"In the beginning"*. We can actually uncover several words embedded within the Hebrew word *Beresheet.*

בראשית *Beresheet* = *"In the Beginning"*.

בראשית *Aish* = "a growing or expanding fire".

בראשית *Resh* = "head", as in the "head" at the beginning and/or the "head" at the leading edge or tip of an expansion.

בראשית *Reshet* = "woven net", as in a fisherman's net that is contracted and squeezed down into the palm of the hand before being cast out into the air as it opens to its fullest extent, much like a web or fractal.

בראשית *Reshe(sh)* = "At the head/leading edge of the rushing headwaters", as in at the leading tip of a rushing expansion, much like surfing.

Viewing *beresheet* in its ancient *Proto Sinaitic* glyph spelling can also be quite a profoundly opening experience unto itself. Proto Sinaitic is a Middle Bronze Age script which we know little about other than its intended letter meanings. The Egyptian alphabets, as well as several less known scripts including Proto Sinaitic, developed as alphabets based on symbols, glyphs and pictograms. Each glyph represented that letter's meaning. These letter meanings were brought directly into the Semitic languages of Aramaic and Hebrew until ultimately falling into disuse by common everyday speakers. The ancient letter meanings were later revived through the mystical philosophies of the kabbalah hundreds of years later.

The following pictograms of the word *beresheet*, or "in the beginning" are to be read from right to left, and they represent the Proto Sinaitic characters of *bet – rash – alp – tsan – yad – taw*, which are the equivalents of the Aramaic and Hebrew *beyt – resh – alef – shin – yod – tau*. These letters embody the meanings of "House" – "Head" – "Ox" – "Tooth" – "Hand" – "Sign".

Now, let's unveil more of the nuances of *beresheet* by going letter by letter.

ב

The first letter *bet* or *beyt* means "house", "break open or out", "burst", "blessing", "with", "within", "through", "express", "inside" or "in the".

Beyt is not simply referring to the frame or the physicality of a house, so much as what I am observing has an appearance of an "inside" and an "outside" – *an appearance of duality.* The first letter *beyt* is where the words "in the" come from. So the first character for the Torah is observing the appearance of an apparent duality – "inside and outside", "light and dark", "positive and negative", "feminine and masculine", "awake and asleep", "before and after", and so on *ad infinitum.* Beyt is the intimate realization of Divine Balance as the open blessing of Life Itself.

ר

The second letter *resh* means "head", "initiate", "radiate", "reaching", "at the head of" as in the *beginning,* while simultaneously meaning "at the head of" as in the "*end*" or "*leading edge*" of a process or an expansion. The "head" at the beginning is also the "head" at the end. The *alef* (first letter of the Hebrew alphabet) and the *tau* – the last letter – are both at "the head". In Hebrew and Aramaic, the *alef* is the *tau.* In Greek, the *alpha* is the *omega.* The "beginning" *is* the "end".

Sayings 18 and 19 of the Coptic Gospel of Thomas sheds a rich light on the Hebrew – Aramaic word *resh,* or "head". I have always sensed a bit of a chuckle in Yeshua's voice as he responded to this fairly innocent inquiry, which, when viewed more deeply, is quite comical by its very nature.

18) The disciples said to Jesus, *"Tell us how our end will be."*
Jesus said, *"Have you discovered, then, the beginning,*
that you look for the end? For where the beginning is,
there will the end be. Blessed is the one who will take his place
in the beginning; for he will know the end and will not taste death."

19) Jesus said, *"Blessed is the one who came into being*
before he came into being."

Again, the ancient Aramaic language had no words to represent the idea of "effect", though they did have several words, such as *saray,* which meant to "visit", to "do" or to "set a process into motion". They did not view "cause" and "effect" as separate things but rather as two qualities of one singular continuum of being. Our belief in a separate cause and effect reveals our inability to see deeply enough into the singular nature of the process of Creation. Why label it as an "effect" if it is in no way separate from its "cause?"

Even more beautifully, when Yeshua was speaking with Judean Pharisee leader *Nicodemus* in John Chapter 3, it is not written in his language that he ever said the words "born again", which is in truth a medieval European Christian concept that is almost perfectly 180 degrees opposite of its original first century Semitic context.

The 1611 King James Bible reads as follows:
"Iesus answered, and said vnto him, Uerily, verily I say vnto thee, except a man be borne againe, he cannot see the kingdome of God."

The Aramaic phrase is quite different:

ܐܡܝܢ ܐܡܝܢ ܐܡܪ
Ahmeyn ahmeyn amar
I am absolutely affirming to you

ܐܢܐ ܠܟ ܕܐܢ ܐܢܫ ܠܐ ܡܬܝܠܕ ܡܢ ܕܪܝܫ
ana lak d'ean anash la metelid man d'rish
that if one is not rebirthed from the *resh*
[*head of the first cause/ beginning or leading edge*]

ܠܐ ܡܫܟܚ ܕܢܚܙܐ ܡܠܟܘܬܗ ܕܐܠܗܐ
la meshkakh d'nekhzea mlkootha d'Alaha
he is not able to comprehend
the Realm of The Absolute, Only Being

Until we realize that the beginning *IS* the end, we cannot realize the singular, unbroken, eternal nature of what we now call "God". In the words of T.S. Eliot's The Four Quartets "*The end precedes the beginning; and the end and the beginning were always there. Before the beginning and after the end.*" Or, in the words of St. Augustine of Hippo, "*God is a circle whose center is everywhere and whose circumference is nowhere.*"

The Aramaic phrase *man d'rish* embodies a dual meaning of "from the head of", as in the "beginning", as well as "from the head", as in the leading edge – the "first is last" and the "last is first". This brings in the ancient nuance of *metelid man d'rish* meaning to be rebirthed "from the head" as also meaning "from above" or the "top of the head" which could also be referencing the opening of the *sahasrara* or "crown chakra". This is the process of awakening the state of pure consciousness in which "the observer and the observed become one". Or again, in the words of St. Francis of Assisi, *"What you are looking for is what is looking"*. The "head" at the beginning is the "head" at the leading edge of the expansion.

The third letter *alef* means "ox", "master" or "all". *Alef* – the first letter of the Semitic alphabets – recognizes that all exists within one singular, non-dual, whole unity of being. *Alef* is the recognition that true power and mastery can come only through the realization of wholeness, or Sacred Unity – as one single unity of being. In essence, there is only the one. Plain and simple. When viewed in light of the first two letters of *beresheet*, we see that although we observe a "bursting out" or apparent duality through the power of the letter *beyt*, we must realize that "the head is the head" and that all exists within the Sacred Unity of the One – *within Itself, as Itself.*

The metaphor of *alef* as an ox goes back many thousands of years to the Akkadian and Sumerian languages and cultures. The ox was widely honored to be the most powerful animal due to the fact that it utilizes so much of its body holistically through its actions. Unlike many animals which may simply have strong arms, legs, haunches or very bodily region specific strength, an ox appears to use ALL of its body as a whole to achieve its unequaled power. The understanding reflected in writings and pictographs of the time was that true power exists only through a state of absolute wholeness – of using the entire body – or entire "body of knowledge, wisdom and experience" – in its entirety. True strength exists not in the individual strength of the "parts", but only within the strength of true wholeness.

The fourth letter *shin* or *sheen* means "tooth", "shine", "express", "gleam", "shimmer", "facet" or "step". The shin is the letter that expresses, shines and shows or makes itself known. Much like a silent potentiality that now speaks forth and steps into its fullest potential as expressions or facets of its own nature made manifest, or obvious. In the beginning was the Word, which is the One expressing Itself in the appearance of layers, facets or steps to become the physical dimension of Creation.

י

The fifth letter *yod* means "Hand", "Will", "Obvious" or "Extension as Self". The *yod* as the "hand" or "will" of the One is succinctly revealed in John 1:3 through the phrase "everything existed through His hands and without him not one thing existed of the things which have existed." The Aramaic phrase "everything existed through His hands" (*kul biaydeh haoeh*) utilizes the Aramaic word *aydeh*, which means "as obvious as the hand" or something that is "an extension as itself". This does not simply mean that "God created everything with His hands", which would be an erroneous effect of anthropomorphizing God into a human. Rather, this means that God IS everything – that what we call "God" is in fact One, that *Alaha* is the Absolute, Only Being, that "God is all that exists." The "extension of everything" IS the One!

The sixth letter *tau* means "sign", "Itself", "mirror" or "reflection". The *tau* is the "mirror" or "reflection" at the "end" of the expansion. It is, in the words of Alan Watts in his book *The Taboo Against Knowing Who You Are* – "the universe looking at itself from billions of points of view." Here are a few examples of how we can bring through the depth of a letter translation of *beresheet* – *beyt, resh, alef, shin, yod, tau* – into modern English:

בראשית

In the
Start
of the All
Expresses
the Will
of Itself
Within
the Initial
Whole
Shining
as (an) Obvious
Reflection–Mirror–Echo–Sign
of Itself

Also, get out a notebook and try a few of your own experiential translations of *beresheet.* And stay tuned, as I am already deep into work on a book that will allow you the opportunity to do your own experiential letter translations!

SECTION THREE

PROCESS: *Vocal Toning as a Spiritual Practice*

"God is not an observer in our lives; God is the *consciousness* of our lives. As we begin to more fully comprehend the constant and abiding presence of Divine Spirit, we will find ourselves entertaining the notion that our every utterance, our every thought and absolutely everything we express into life is a calling out to God.

Every time we curse, we are praying. Every time we are angry, we are praying. Every time someone tells a joke, or laughs, or lies, or cries, what is happening is prayer. Our judgments are prayers. Our fears and phobias are prayers. Spirit is present in the midst of it all. Everything we think, say and do is a prayer, and every bit of it is having a direct and significant effect on our lives."

REV. DR. JOHN WATERHOUSE
From the book "*Five Steps to Freedom*"
[DeVorss]

CHAPTER 12

FROM ANCIENT TONES TO MODERN LANGUAGE

There is a part of me that wants to just pull you headfirst into the water and start laying out each of the letters in the Aramaic and Hebrew alphabets and their development from written pictographs to their more modern letters. For now, though, I do want to lay a secure base for you to at least feel a much more rewarding experience in the knowing that these spoken human sounds are not just happenstance *wu wu* mystical nonsense. Unfortunately, though, some who have not taken the time to study very many other languages outside of Aramaic and Hebrew may be quick to label it exactly that.

The modern written forms of the Syriac, Aramaic and Hebrew alphabets embody the echoes of roots that go back many millennia into the ancient world. The ancient letter meanings have long since faded into the background in the pursuit of the much more colloquial, common everyday words meanings. Some literalists even discount these written letter meanings as being nothing more than much later Kabbalistic metaphor. Beware when you hear this because what it actually reveals is an immense lack of study on the part of the accuser.

I am the last person who will ever call myself an "expert" on anything. I just want to be *open* to receive a greater Truth, right here and right now, in this present moment. Though it was not fully formalized until much later, the basis of *Kabbalah* pre-dates the first official Holy

Bible by well over a thousand years. Much like Kabbalah, *Sufism,* although it has thrived as a mystical vine of Islam, actually predates Islam by well over a thousand years.

I do not exemplify my awareness simply by obsessing about what is "*on the page*", but rather by how fully I am essentially *living* these insights in my own spiritual life. Put simply, if I am not actualizing and embodying the deepest sense of what these insights actually *mean* through the direct experience of living them on a day to day, moment by moment basis, then I am doing nothing more than revealing my own lack of understanding of what these teachings actually *mean*, outside of their accepted "*definitions*". Just because we can define a word does not in any way imply that we actually know what it *means.* It is time for us to step out of the classroom and actually *live it!*

The issue can get somewhat complicated due to the fact that Aramaic can be quite an elusive language and in truth rare enough that some folks may actually make up just about whatever they want in relation to it. Another common issue is that many people "teaching" spiritual insights from the Aramaic Yeshua story are often simply repackaging the works of others – especially from *Dr Rocco Errico*, *Dr. George Lamsa* and *Saadi Neil Douglas-Klotz* – without doing much, if any, of their own research and development in the field. Again, just because we have memorized a theological definition or biblical verse does not in any way whatsoever mean that we know what it *means* in its deepest essence. While it is great that the Aramaic perceptive is getting out there into the world, we must give credit where credit is due and acknowledge those trailblazers who have gone before us. I am deeply honored and grateful to stand on the shoulders of giants.

This is compounded by the reality that some widely embraced modern "*translations of the words of Jesus*" are more often profound poetic renderings *inspired* by the literal Aramaic words themselves. I have personally taken a lot of heat myself for this over the two decades of my Aramaic studies and work because much of my teachings often fit into this category. This occurs irrespective of the fact that I am continually stating that a perfect, literal translation is not even possible the instant that we part the veil below the top level, obvious *peshat* literal definitions of a word or phrase.

Clearly, if the Yeshua teachings were intended to be taken literally, then why on earth would he so often speak in parables? My work does not lie in the literal translations, but rather in unpacking the widest breadth of possible nuance in the experiential meanings of the teachings when they are put into practice and *lived.* It is time to burn down the conceptual fences of theology so that we can responsibly begin to reveal the mythic archetypes concealed beneath the literal face of the Jesus story.

The matter can get even further problematic due to these poetic renderings often being so incredibly inspiring and heart opening that people immediately jump on the boat and declare that "*this is what Jesus REALLY said!*" The hard truth is that we do not know if Jesus actually said a single word of any of these teachings because we were not there, leaving all reincarnation references aside. Literal translation of the "words of Jesus" is simply not possible and we need to remain accountable and forthcoming with this reality.

It must also be said that in order to fully communicate the deeper aspects of the Yeshua teachings, one must have at least some degree of direct, intimate experience in the states of consciousness and awareness which Yeshua was so obviously pointing toward – *eyes that see and ears that hear* – yet this absolutely vital and indispensable base is so often swept aside in a mad pursuit of being "right". As I so often say, there is no right or wrong, only educated opinions and hypotheses. However, I am much more apt to move along a path that is willing to actually put these teachings into practice rather than the much safer, less-accountable decision to simply study and talk *about* them. The rubber must "hit the road" before one can objectify the deepest truth of these eternal cosmic philosophies, without exception.

That is not to say that these renderings do not have deeply significant value in modern linguistic scholarship of ancient philosophies. Regardless, some modern authorities are very quick to denounce these poetic renderings as simply contemporary fabrications cashing in on the *chicness* of the Aramaic words of Jesus in modern times. This may be the case for some. What is happening appears to be the development of two sides to one single coin, despite efforts by a select few of us to "agree to disagree".

In my view, both are absolutely essential, though I will definitely say that the "mystics" would be much quicker to acknowledge and praise the essential value of scientific linguistic research than many self-aggrandized "real" experts would be willing to acknowledge the heart-opening, practical hands-on work of "not so real" mystics. We seek to keep our hearts open and continue to reach out in gratitude and honor for the immense work of those in the trenches of linguistics and scientific language and cultural studies. We mystics could simply not do what we do without their efforts.

As I mentioned earlier, my experience with being on the receiving end of such intense, harsh criticism has brought me into the empathetic understanding that if someone is coming after me or anyone else from a place of fear, hostility and harsh judgment, then they obviously either do not understand, or are simply not living the very heart of the teachings that they espouse. They very likely do not even know what the heart of those teachings even is. I have come to realize that if someone is able to attack the work of another, then their opinion is not one that I would care to waste my time with anyway. Put simply, if they actually knew what they were talking about, then they would be *living* it with their heart rather than attacking someone else with their apparent, selective "knowledge".

Harsh attacks and discernment are not in any way the same thing. Though we all "lose it" from time to time, if we are in a regular attack mode, this reveals nothing more than a fear of not grasping the core of whatever philosophy we are attempting to jam down someone else's throat. We must release and remove the temptation to bite the hook from within our own heart. Cultivating a practice of proactive vulnerability has kept me in touch with the open space of my being. I have learned to do my best in each moment to honor and respect all perspectives, to emanate compassion and send them love and blessings. Then I move on.

I have learned to fully embrace my labeling as a *heretic*, which comes from the ancient Koine Greek word *heresis*, which meant "to choose". Sign me up, because I am most definitely a card-carrying heretic! While rigid orthodoxy may at times feel safe, it is most often nothing more than a reassuring structure of comfort. Not because it is necessarily more accurate, but rather because it is so clearly defined, accepted and "time tested". However, the world was once so obviously flat, was it not? And did the entire universe not rotate around the cosmic epicenter of earth? Um, no, not at all. These errors happened only on the level of conceptual, widely held and accepted belief.

It is your own personal choice to walk the path that feels right for *you*. I know many who have stayed clearly within the well-traveled road of Orthodox religion and these can be some of the most beautiful, loving souls that I have ever encountered. Just like anything though, we can always find under-ripe or over-ripe fruit no matter where we choose to look. You will very likely find whatever it is that you are looking for, be it positive or negative in your judgment. We are each at a point of personal choice. To each their own.

Dr. Albert LaChance often says that "*it is time for the scholars to shut up and let the mystics speak*", and I could not agree more. But this phantom door also swings both ways. It is time for all of us to grow up and come together and actually begin to *live these teachings*, rather than simply falling back on pre-established, ideological frameworks of the "real" and "proven" meanings of these words and sounds. Again, *being able to define a word does not in any way necessitate you knowing what it actually means.* I believe that the key to finding our true balance lies somewhere in the middle.

I very clearly see, much like Yeshua, that true life comes not simply from what is clearly "known", but rather maybe even more so from the Great Mystery, from the vast expanse of *non-knowing*, from the clear, pure depth of that we do *NOT* know. We must remain open to those eternal forces which do not fit within our very limited idea of five senses of taste, touch, smell, sight and hearing. The echoing voice of eternity is not heard with the ear but rather felt with the heart. In truth, even our five commonly accepted senses is a misnomer, as psychology has long embraced twenty-one or more individual and unique human senses. Yet the "fact" of only five human senses lives on as a modern folklore.

A strong case in point would be the study of the ancient letter meanings which ultimately morphed into the common Aramaic and Hebrew words that so many fight over the meanings of. Despite the immense wealth of research, study, evidence and overwhelming documentation of the evolution of ancient spoken sounds being originally written as pictographs or glyphs to reveal their perceived meanings, modern scholarship all but ignores this aspect and rests almost entirely on the words themselves, rather than the sound components within these words.

Modern scholars like *Stan Tenen* of the *Meru Foundation*, as well as *Neil Douglas-Klotz*, have endured immense criticism of their revelations about the much deeper meanings embodied within the letters, glyphs and the sounds themselves, rather than simply in the everyday words that these letters are puzzle pieces within. As soon as someone ventures outside of the pre-established patterns of what appears to be "obvious" to a pre-conditioned expert within any scientific field of study, they are often almost immediately attacked for their arrogance and preposterous claims about something that has, up to this stage, been locked within an ideological structure of comfort.

Put simply, as I have said before in this book, we need to grow up, take a few steps back, and to allow the Jesus story to grow up as well. Let's stop projecting a stagnant, virtually lifeless dogma onto these ancient philosophies and instead embrace the possibility that we have yet to even begin to scratch through the outer surface of the widest possible breadth of what these transformational teachings could possibly mean, regardless of their homogeneous, widely-accepted literal meanings. If we rest in literality then we shall surely choke out the very last breath of life within even the most widely loved and embraced spiritual teachings of the ages. It is so much easier to just talk *about* something than it is to actually *do it* and *live it*, isn't it?

In relation to toning these ancient sounds and words, the key lies not in having a thorough intellectual understanding of what these sounds are believed to *mean*, so much as in simply *doing it.* As I continue to say, the key to toning lies embedded within the process itself, and not in our understanding of it. In the end, regardless of what we do or do not believe about any great philosophy, if we are not actually living it, then it means virtually nothing. I am not asking you to tone these sounds with the intention of "recognizing" what they "really" mean so much as asking you to simply tone these sounds and let yourself be curious and open in the process itself. So let's dive in now and give toning a try!

Chapter 13

Experimenting with Pure Tones

I do my best in my Aramaic toning circles to focus on the very important understanding that the true power of vocal toning does not lie in flawless technique, a great voice, perfect pronunciation or anything other than simply doing it with an open heart and mind. The real magic of toning is in the process itself and not in any predetermined rules or steps that we should be following. Though I am revealing the ancient Near Eastern Aramaic Gnostic nuance of meaning within these words and sounds, that does not in any way mean that the Aramaic meanings are correct and those of another language are wrong.

I often explain these variances in cultural and linguistic meanings of the same words and sounds as multiple people observing a large, shimmering, multifaceted diamond from numerous points of view. In other words, how could we NOT observe our personal experiences of the same object of perception differently? Within this understanding lies the greatest depth of potential experience through the process of vocal toning. Again, the spark lies in our openness to the direct experience of the tones themselves. Let go, at least in the beginning, of any need to define or put descriptive words to your experience and instead *just do it.*

The most immediately productive way to introduce toning to a newbie is to begin by toning pure vowel sounds such as *aye*, *ee*, *eye*, *oh* and *oo*. The key here is, again, not in perfect pronunciation or enunciation, but rather in our willingness to be open to the direct experience of the sound itself. Even after two decades of consciously toning as a spiritual practice, I myself do not tone to recognize or observe some pre-defined meaning or quality of the sound I am toning. I simply open myself mindfully into the experience and begin toning while remaining open and aware of how I *feel*. It is literally that simple. Overcomplicating the toning process will not offer us a better experience, but rather just a more mental, intellect-based one.

Another very important thing to understand is that the pitch or tone that resonates well for me will not necessarily be the pitch that resonates well for you. If I were to sit James Earl Jones beside Celine Dion, I am quite positive that the pitch that would light James Earl up would be quite lower than the frequency that would feel the most comfortable for Celine. When I offer toning circles with large groups of people, I make sure that everyone present knows that it is not important that they are nailing the pitch exactly as I am toning it.

What is most important is that we allow ourselves to be as open in the toning experience as we can be in this present moment. It is not a perfectly manifest sound or tone that is essential, but rather the tone or presence of our awareness as the tone is birthing *through* us that matters. So let go of perfection and open yourself up to presence. Allow this awareness of the power of vocal toning to be the base of your experience when beginning your practice. Again, it is not about the clearly defined meaning of the words or sounds so much as it is about being open to the direct experience of the pure vibration itself.

Toning for the First Time

To begin, sit, stand or lie flat in a comfortable, balanced position. Close your eyes and spend a few moments reintegrating within the present moment. Take three deep cleansing breaths. Breathe in through your nose, hold it in your lungs for a few moments, and then exhale fully through your mouth. Visualize yourself breathing in the *hayye* or *chi* – the vital life essence – and hold that energy in your body temple for a few moments and then exhale, releasing all thought, concerns and mental patterns. *Just let go*. Do this three times.

Again, allow yourself to be fully aware of this present moment as you sit in silence for a minute or so. Now, begin toning the sound *ahhhhhhhhhhhhhh*, like the short "o" sound in "God", in a pitch that feels comfortable to you within your vocal range. Tone the *ah* sound several times, leaving a few moments in between tones to refill your lungs with fresh air before moving on to the next *ah*.

Be open within the awareness of how the sound *feels* within you, not only in an elusive "spiritual" manner, but literally *feeling* the tone somatically in your physical body itself. After toning the sound several times back to back for several minutes, allow yourself to simply sit in silence and observe the echoing vibrations that continue to reverberate throughout your body temple. Be curious and open within the experience.

Try this same process again with some of these sounds that follow before moving on to the next chapter of toning the *Ancient Aramaic words of Yeshua*. I will go much deeper in future books about the ancient meanings of these ancient root sounds, though at this point in your process, you will be best served with less definition and more openness to the direct experiential *feeling* of these sounds within the toning process. Again, there is no magic key or instruction here other than allowing ourselves to be fully open within the toning process itself. Just be open and curious.

aye as in "bay"

ee as in "sleep"

eye as is "eye"

oh as in "no"

oo as in "you"

rah as is "rock"

ma as in "mama"

gah as in "god"

shhh as in "sheep"

Chapter 14

Toning the Ancient Aramaic Words of Yeshua

So that the reader is fully informed, I have chosen not to utilize the currently accepted, though frequently evolving pronunciation and transliteration keys employed by most linguists. I have learned over the course of two decades of public teaching experience with tens of thousands of people that the everyday seeker learns much more efficiently when offered a very clear and streamlined instruction on how to pronounce the words we will be toning. The learning curve is most often far too immense for me to take this method of teaching pronunciations seriously for the casual student.

In the scientific study of languages, these generally accepted, fairly universal pronunciation keys are absolutely essential and virtually indispensable, so as to maintain some sense of universality when moving from one language to another. For our general purposes however, we will not need them at this stage of the process. I will instead be using common English words and pronunciation examples that can be easily understood by those seekers dipping their toes into the water for the first time.

This choice is very important in my intent to make this process of toning as universal and easy to grasp by as many people as possible. A past challenge for myself and many others has been buying a book on toning or on the healing power of sound, only to be bombarded by overly complex, excessively technical examples of sounds and pronunciations that would have served us much more efficiently if expressed in a state of humility and simplicity. In this section we will begin toning a few of the actual Aramaic words that are attributed to Yeshua. My goal is to keep this book focused in on a clean, clear and easy to pronounce and understand base before launching off into complex mantras and phrases.

Begin by sitting or lying down in a comfortable, balanced position. Close your eyes and spend a few moments reintegrating within the present moment. Take three deep cleansing breaths. Breathe in through your nose, hold it in your lungs for a few moments, and then exhale fully through your mouth. Visualize yourself breathing in the *hayye* or *chi* – the vital life essence – and hold that energy in your body temple for a few moments, and then exhale, releasing all thought, concerns and mental patterns. Do this three times before toning each sound.

<u>ABWOON</u>

KJV: *"Our Father"*

EXPERIENTIAL ARAMAIC INTERPRETATION:
"Our One, Absolute Eternal Being, through which we are borne forth"

LETTER TRANSLATION:
"The Whole One burst open as blessing within Itself to expand through its conscious connection [within Itself] as its own multiplicity of manifestations [within Itself]"

SUGGESTED TONING: *ah–oon*

Abwoon, or *ah-oon* as I most often tone it, is the Aramaic word that I most often begin my toning circles with because it embodies a vibrational quality that is immediately felt as it is being toned. There is simply no denying it. *Abwoon* sets a strong base of presence upon which the remainder of an experiential gathering can be built. *Abwoon* feels great and is easily the word that I tone most often throughout my day. I also often begin my talks with a group toning of *abwoon* to open our hearts and set the space for what is to come.

In my gatherings, I often use *abwoon* to help illuminate how we can reveal layers of meaning within a sacred word. *Abwoon* is the first word of the Aramaic "Lord's Prayer" from the gospels of *Mattai* and *Luqa* (Matthew and Luke). This prayer is also commonly referred to as the "*Our Father*" because of its beginning "*Our Father who art in Heaven*" in common translations. *Abwoon* is the Eternal Wellspring of Life Itself and the presence of true wholeness which creates and gives birth from, into and through the expansive force of *Alaha – The One, Absolute, Only, Eternal Being. Abwoon* consistently births anew from absolute to manifest.

The common colloquial meaning of *abwoon* is simply "*Our Father*". Not much magic there, but it does summon up the awareness of a parental figure through which we are born. In fact, Dr. Rocco Errico translates *abwoon* as "*Our Parent*" and Dr. Michael Ryce brings it through as "*Our Eternal Creator*". The *aleph bet* or *"ab"* sound means *"father"* or "parent" or "source" and the *waw nun* letter combination – the sound *oon* – means "*everyone*" or "*all*". An example would be the word *touveyhoun*, translated at the beginning of each of Yeshua's beatitudes from the Gospel of Matthew as "*blessed are*" or, more accurately "*blessed are all of you*". The *oon* suffix is the meaning of "*all of you are*". So we have the literal "*Our Father*".

The letter *aleph* at the beginning of *abwoon* means "*everything*", "*all*" or "*all exists within the rooted strength of one single, unity or process*". Literally, only one. The second *beyt* letter signifies an appearance of an "*inside and outside*" and a "*bursting open as its own blessing*". Of course, when viewed in harmony with the first *aleph*, this "*bursting open as its own blessing*" is happening *within itself.* The third *waw* letter represents action, much like the *ing* suffix in English. Its ancient meaning is "*pins*", "*spine*", "*replication*" and "*multiplicity*". The *waw* sound signifies a process of a fractal expansion, much like the outward radiation of light rays from the center point of the sun. The final letter *nun* represents the "*connection*" or "*completion of a circle*" as well as the "*neck connected to the head or outermost edge of an expansion*", as in the multiplicity of all manifestation.

RA

EXPERIENTIAL ARAMAIC INTERPRETATION:
"Obvious, masculine, manifest light"

LETTER TRANSLATION:
"From its source [head] to its leading edge [head] within the wholeness of Itself"

SUGGESTED TONING: *rah*

Toning the ancient sound *ra* is one of the most expansive, opening experiences that I have ever felt while toning. When toning this word, you may very likely feel a very strong, pronounced, expansive energetic "opening" in the third eye and crown chakras. This is due, I believe, not only to the power of the sounds themselves, but also as part of the intimate relationship of our energy bodies to the wide-open vibrational quality of the *ra* sound.

Ra is a very ancient tone in a multitude of languages that signifies a "*shining forth of heat and light*". It was one of the Egyptian words for "*sun*" as well as a reference to the only-begotten the sun god of Egypt. The solar messiah philosophy was ultimately merged with the mythic sun god *Horus*, circa 3000 BC, who was also called the "*only begotten son of God*". *Horus*, who was born of the virgin *Isis-Mary*, was also known as *Ra.*

Ra was one of the most often toned sounds in the mystery schools of ancient Egypt. We know this because implicit instructions for doing so are etched into ancient temple walls, as well as recorded in numerous texts. This simple, yet energetically rich tone was consciously drawn up the *central pillar*, or *chakra system* throughout the process of *tantric energetic alchemy*. Yeshua spoke in Chapter Three of the Gospel of John about Moses having "raised up the serpent in the desert". The ancient Aramaic word translated in John 3:14 as "desert" is pronounced *mid-bar*. Yeshua raised the serpent, known in Sanskrit as *kundalini*, up the mid-bar. The Aramaic word for serpent is *khooyah*, which means "energy force" or "life energy."

The Syriac Aramaic Gnostic text of *The Gospel of Mary*, also known as *The Gospel According to Mary Magdalene*, references the secret teaching of drawing awareness up through the "powers" or "energies" of the life temple. Mary even details the energetic quality of each of the seven chakras when they are shut down and not "speaking freely". These seven unopened energy centers were translated as *daimonia*, or "demons" in Koine Greek.

In chapter sixteen of the Aramaic Gospel of Mark, the words used for what was translated into Greek as "cast out seven demons" is *shabea sheadeyn apeq*. *Shabea* is the Aramaic word for the number seven. *Apeq* means "*to stimulate or exercise the movement of*" and *sheadeyn*, translated as "devils" or "demons" means "*unopened energies or spirits*" and "*spirits or forces not voicing freely*". This almost comical misunderstanding of the seven unopened energy centers of the body has incited nearly four dozen versions of the "*seven deadly sins or vices*", as many religious authorities have exercised a tremendous amount of artistic license for nearly 2,000 years. In fact, many bibles end with Chapter Fifteen of the Gospel of Mark, deleting the seven energy centers out completely.

The *ra* tone is by far the most intensively profound tone for opening the energy centers of the body temple. Words that end with the sound *ra* or *ah* are some of the most powerfully transformational and "*socket frying*" of all tones. Try toning *ra* and see for yourself!

RAKHMA

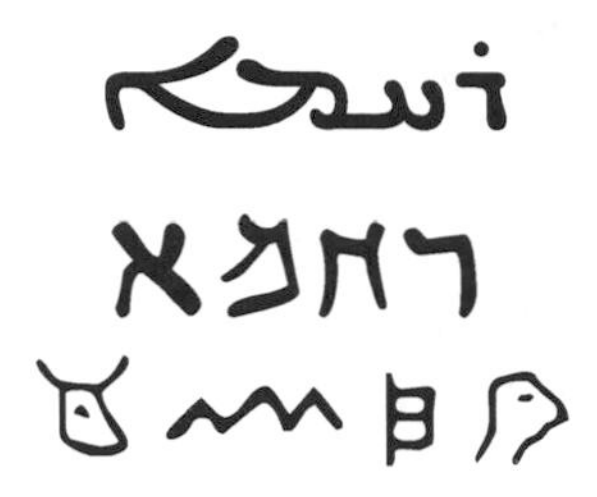

KJV: *"Merciful", "Mercy","Friend"*

EXPERIENTIAL ARAMAIC INTERPRETATION:
"A shining forth of conscious light and heat birthing from the inner womb of being"

LETTER TRANSLATION:
"From its own [head] to its leading edge [head] encompassing the great, flowing expanse within the wholeness of Itself"

SUGGESTED TONING: *rah–mah*

Rakhma is the all-Embracing love for another. *Rakhma* is a realization that what we call "love" is not a commodity or "thing" which can be given or taken, but rather what we *ARE* when living and communicating from the deepest spaciousness within our being. *Rakhma* is the all-encompassing, all-embracing Love which flows forth from the Center Point of one's True Being.

As I mentioned earlier, the *ra* sound, which is present in dozens of ancient languages, points toward an expansive radiating forth of heat and light. The Old Hebrew root sound *khm* represents a re-birthing process and a "quaking" which radiates from one's "inner womb". *Rakhma* surrounds, includes, nurtures, feeds, and stimulates vibrant, vital Life and growth in all who are embraced by and through it while instantaneously burning off anything unlike pure, all-encompassing love in one's consciousness. *Rakhma* is also a word for "*friend*". *Rama,* which is how we most often tone this sound, is also one of the primary "Lords" in Sanskrit Vaishnava Hinduism.

I could quite easily write on and on for pages about the incredibly deep, multi-layered nuances of meaning in the deeply experiential term *rakhma.* I have been told by native Assyrian Aramaic Christians that *rakhma* is the most precious jewel of wisdom, love and consciousness that must be guarded vigilantly, though they do not know "what it is". We know *rakhma* not by its factual, academic colloquial definitions but rather by the radiance of its expanding light within the deepest recesses of our being.

Rakhma is the dancing vibrations of life essence that I felt when I first looked into the eyes of my three children within seconds of their births as I held those living, breathing beings of vibrant light in my arms. *Rakhma* is the palpable presence of conscious life threaded within the midst of my beautiful mother's passing life in her final moments here on earth. *Rakhma* is the quaking, spiritually seismic shift in the energy field of a mother who, having not seen her estranged child or loved one for many years, now comes into the direct experience of embracing that child in her arms.

Rakhma is the shining presence of light and heat that radiates forth from the center point of our true being in the moments following a true inner forgiveness process, when we have literally "*removed the root of our suffering*" and, as a result, can perceive the presence of this moment clearly. Though needing to define the most complex book-learned definitions of *rakhma* would be a gross exposure of our spiritual immaturity, there is one thing that I do know without reservation: *Rakhma* is the natural, ever expanding light of our true being.

Noohra

ܢܘܗܪܐ

נוהרא

𐤍𐤅𐤄𐤓𐤀

KJV: *"Light"*

Experiential Aramaic Interpretation:
"Conscious, reflective, feminine light of awareness"

Letter Translation:
"The connecting consciousness of its own expansion through the window from its source [head] to its leading edge [head] within the wholeness of Itself"

Suggested Toning: *noo–rah*

Noohra is the ancient Aramaic word representing the "*conscious, reflective, feminine light of human awareness*". Noohra is also the word for the feminine, reflective light of *sahara* – the moon. In the ancient Semitic, as well as Egyptian, Sumerian, Akkadian and Phoenician philosophies, the light of human consciousness is a feminine reflection of the *light of God's son*, just as the light of the moon is a feminine reflection of the light of *shemsha* – the physical sun, commonly called "*God's sun*" or the "*only sun of God.*" These were very common, everyday outlooks on human awareness and our place within the one and only Light of Life Itself.

I often laugh at the uneducated, modern declaration of "*I don't believe in astrology because I read the Bible!*" My first response is "*have you ever actually read the Bible?*" Astrology is everywhere, from beginning to end and everywhere in between, especially in the words attributed to Yeshua.

However, unlike the way astrology has developed largely in our present times as an ideology or belief system, in ancient times the cosmology of the stars and planets and celestial bodies and our place within it was not simply a mental credence, it was the way of life itself.

With the sound *noohra*, we are adding the sound *noo* or *new* to the tone *ra*. Of course, in English, new means "fresh" or "unique". The intriguing insight we are offered here is that the reflected light of the moon is not new or fresh at all, but in truth simply the reflected light of the sun. The same can be said of human awareness and human light. Our consciousness is in truth the reflected light of eternity itself. Again, "*What you are looking for is what is looking.*"

MAARYAH

ܡܪܝܐ

מריא

𐤌𐤓𐤉𐤀

KJV: *"Lord"*

EXPERIENTIAL ARAMAIC INTERPRETATION:
"One who shines forth feminine light from a place of strength"

LETTER TRANSLATION:
"Expressing the great, flowing expanse from its source [head] to its leading edge [head] extending [itself] outward from within its strength in wholeness"

SUGGESTED TONING: *mah–ree-ah*

Very few realize that the 1611 King James term *lord* was created in medieval England through feudalism and did not even exist during the time of Yeshua. In ancient Aramaic culture, the word *maryah* was used to recognize one who "*shines a feminine spiritual light from a place of strength*" and was never a description of one person's earthly power over another. Another much more common, colloquial Aramaic word *mari* was also more of term of endearment than the acknowledgement of a power person or *lord* in the sense that we often think of it today.

The primary Greek word for lord is *kyrios*, which was also a term used when speaking of *Zeus*, the greatest of the Greek pantheon of Gods. Incidentally, the ancient Koine Greek word *Iesous,* the source of the word "*Jesus*" in truth means "*hail Zeus*". I will also admit that I do shudder a bit when I hear someone say *Jeshua*, as there is no "J" sound in Aramaic. The letter J has in fact only been around for a few hundred years in ANY language.

The co-dependent, medieval English feudal term *lord* was widely used in the original 1611 "authorized" King James Bible and continues to be heavily used to this day. Few actually sit and think about the significance of this word on modern sensibilities, not to mention how far removed it is from its much more ancient tonality and meaning. The feudal lord, or land owner, was also called the "bread giver" or the "giver of life" by the peons, or general laborers within feudalism.

The ancient root sounds of *ray*, *reya*, *reeah* and *aura* all point toward an expanding feminine, reflective light that is *sensed* more than seen. Much like the human aura or etheric energy fields, we are speaking of a light that is not easily seen by the human eye, but rather sensed through the open space of the mystical heart. The Greek word *mystikol* points toward something that is directly experiential rather than only cognitively understood. The *mar* sound connotes a firm bedrock of strength which exists in a state of absolute wholeness or *holiness*.

The etymology of the *yah* sound is hotly debated in scholarly circles. While some claim that *yah* at the end of *maryah* points to *"Yah"*, or YHWH, many refute that claim in light of the fact that the *ya* sound in *maryah* is derived from the Hebrew/Aramaic letters *yod* and *alef* rather than *yod* and *hey*, as *yah* is spelled. In either case, *maaryah* can be one of the most powerfully opening tones of the ancient Aramaic words of Yeshua. I particularly love to vary the pitch and intensity while toning *maaryah*, beginning lower and more gently before ultimately building up to my higher registers with much more of a wide open, "peeling back the layers" quality, before basking in an extended post-toning silence.

ROOKHA

ܪܘܚܐ

רוחא

𐤓𐤅𐤇𐤀

KJV: *"Spirit", "Wind"*

EXPERIENTIAL ARAMAIC INTERPRETATION:
"An invisible, yet tangible creative elemental force of Alaha – the Absolute, Only Being"

LETTER TRANSLATION:
"From its source [head] to its leading edge [head] fractally expanding to encompass the wholeness of Itself"

SUGGESTED TONING: *roo–ah*

Rookha are the active, expansive forces within Alaha – the Absolute, Only Being. The ancient Aramaic word *rookha* is a feminine gendered term, though it was translated into Greek as the gender-neutral *pneuma* and into Latin as the masculine *spiritus.* Though this gender modification may not seem all that important on the surface, it is actually quite significant. The neutered Greek *pneuma* would be much closer to the original feminine Aramaic *rookha* than that of the masculine Latin *spiritus. Pneuma* is most often translated as "*spirit*" or "*breath*", though its ancient Koine Greek meaning is closer to "*underlying substance*".

Let's look at a few examples of how changing the gender of a word in fact changes its meaning. First of all, breathe out onto your forearm. What do you feel on your skin? Your breath, right? *Are you sure?*

What you feel on your arms is the masculine gendered Latin *spiritus.* Masculine connotes something physical or *manifest.* Our modern idea of breath is something that we can feel and perceive with our five senses. Thinking of breath in such as way could also include the Greek term *pneuma*, or "*underlying substance*", since *pneuma* is so elusively defined and gender neutral.

One of the problems we have is that when we think of the words *spirit* and *breath*, we think of two different things without realizing that the first century near Eastern mind had not yet clearly divided these two perceptions as being somehow separate from each other. Spirit is breath and breath is spirit. In fact, the Latin root *inspire* ultimately became the Old French term *inspiration*, which found its way into modern English as "*filling with spirit*" and "*breathing*". These two separate *breath* and *spirit* terms are still somewhat connected, though by gendering them masculine, we begin to view them as two different things.

The ancient Aramaic *rookha* is significantly subtler than this. In the ancient Aramaic mind, what you felt on your arm was not breath, but rather hot air. *Rookha* is not a masculine, manifest, physical *thing*, or breath as we think of it today, but rather *our feminine perception of its movement.* Take a deep breath and really let this shift occur in your awareness. *Rookha*, or "*breath*" in the ancient Aramaic sense, is not the hot air that we feel on our arm, but rather *our feminine, reflective perception of its "force" or movement!*

Yeshua was not speaking of breath and spirit as only physical manifestations, but rather of our *perception* of its expansion, retraction and movement. If we are able to be completely honest about our modern western perception of spirit, even though we say with our words that spirit is "not a thing", deep in our beliefs, we still continue to look for it with our physical senses. We must realize that the first century near Eastern Semitic mind, and especially within the Jesus teachings would not have artificially separated breath and spirit from each other.

The Khabouris Codex Foundation says that *rookha* represents "*various invisible but material forces such as wind, magnetism, and electricity*" as well as "*cosmic expansion*", "*gravity*" and now "*nuclear forces*". Herein lies the key to the realization of breath and spirit as our *perception* of these eternal forces, rather than the forces themselves. *Rookha* applies to any elemental force whose source is undetectable but has effects that can be detected through our senses. A similar Hindu word would be *prana.*

Yeshua made this very clear when speaking to Nicodemus, a leader of the Judeans, in the Gospel of John. I wrote earlier in Chapter 11 about the original Aramaic meaning of what is erroneously referred to today as being "*born again*". When viewed in its original language, the phrase *metelid man d'rish* means born "*from the first start*", "*from the beginning*", "*from the head of*" or "*from the leading edge [head]*".

Several lines later, it is written that Yeshua said that if one is not born of what the King James Bible translates as "*water and spirit*", then he cannot "*enter into the Kingdom of God*". The Aramaic is much more deeply nuanced. First of all, the Aramaic word for "*water*" is *maya*, which means not simply "*water*" but also *"vast expanse"*, as also used in the word *shemaya*, translated as "*heaven*", "*sky*" or *"vast expanse."* The first letter in the word *maya* is *mem* literally means "*water*" or *"vast expanse"* and the *aya* sound points toward something with no boundaries, i.e. "*no beginning or ending*", meaning *everywhere* or *everything.* Of course, the word *maya* is also a Hindu and Buddhist word for "*the ever flowing world of liquid illusion*".

I have wondered how Yeshua would have spoken the word *rookha* if he did make this statement. How would he say it to mean "*spirit*" in a way that Nicodemus would comprehend? Do you honestly think that maybe Yeshua flailed his arms wildly in the air as he said *rookha* to demonstrate our modern understanding of *spirit*? If you read the entirety of John Chapter 3, you will very clearly see that Nicodemus was not the most spiritually awake guy in the world.

I do not believe that Yeshua would have intended *rookha* as simply some sort of elusive thing that we can't quite get our arms around in our mental comprehension. I believe that Yeshua very likely would have taken an obvious, intentional breath to drive his point home in a way that even Nicodemus could not mistake. We must be born from the first start of the great, flowing expanse (*maya*) and the eternal forces of all creation (*rookha*).

Yeshua went on to say that the "*wind* (*rookha*) *blows where it will*" and that we do not know where it is coming from or where it is going to, though we can hear its "*voice*", or perceive its effects with our senses. He continued by saying "*as it is for one who is born from rookha*". Remember, breath and spirit were not yet two different, clearly defined "things" back then, but rather nuances of perception in one's direct experience.

A great exercise to try is to take an old bible and everywhere you see the word *"spirit"* in Yeshua's teachings, cross it out with a pencil and write *"breath"* above it. This will give you a much more accurate, directly experiential understanding of what the word *rookha* would have represented in that time. It is not that it does not mean spirit, but rather, its more intimate meaning of breath can be so much more profoundly actualized through one's own conscious experience. Breath is spirit and spirit is breath. Neither are masculine "things" but rather feminine *perceptions.*

<u>AHMEYN</u>

KJV: *"Amen", "Verily", "Assuredly"*

EXPERIENTIAL ARAMAIC INTERPRETATION:
"Consciously flowing forth from the absolute, rooted ground of being"

LETTER TRANSLATION:
"The strength of its own wholeness flows forth from the vast expanse of its extension as itself consciously connected to itself"

SUGGESTED TONING: *ah–main* OR *ah–meen*

The root sound *iman* is the primary word for "*faith*" in Arabic today. *Iman* has long been thought to be derived from a Coptic Egyptian root sound, though deeper studies have been revealing that the *iman* sound we have long thought was brought into Aramaic from Coptic was very likely brought from ancient Aramaic into Coptic some time prior to what has previously been believed.

The tri-consonant root of the letters *alef, mem* and *nun* – the *amn* sound – pivots upon a meaning of "*absolute*", "*firm, rooted earth*", "*rooted center*", "*pivotal importance*" and "*cubit*". What, then, would be the common thread of meaning which runs through all four of these possible definitions? They are all "absolute" in their observation! The firm, rooted earth beneath our feet is absolute. The rooted center of a *galilee* – the ancient Aramaic and Hebrew word for *spinning wheel* – is absolute. And how about cubit? Cubit was an absolute perception of measurement, as in "*this brick is absolutely one cubit*". The inherent quality of the word *ahemyn* is that it is an affirmation of absoluteness, of a movement emanating from an absolute, true rooted center.

Very few Christians have any awareness that the word ultimately translated in the King James Bible as "*verily*" or "*assuredly*" was in truth the Aramaic word *ahmeyn*. It is written that Yeshua would say *ahmeyn* before statements that he was seeking to create a "*fertile root*" into someone's perception with the statement he was about to make. Of course, placing *ahmeyn* at the end of Aramaic and Hebrew prayers goes back long before the lifetime of Yeshua. Even more revealing to what Yeshua may have been seeking to convey is that the ancient Aramaic texts show that Yeshua would often say *ahmeyn* twice before making a statement of affirmation to drive his words even deeper into the fertile, rooted earth center of his listener's memory and awareness.

Why *ahmeyn* was so profoundly diluted in the King James Bible as simply "*verily*" or "*assuredly*" is anyone's guess. *Verily* is derived from the 14th century Middle English word *verray*, meaning simply "*certainly*". *Assuredly*, also a 14th century Middle English word, has the same meaning. Coming into a deeper relationship with the realization that Yeshua was in truth saying *ahmeyn, ahmeyn* can help open our hearts to a much more experiential, inner experience of many of his deepest affirmations within his teachings. We would be much closer with the words "*sealed within and through the absolute, rooted ground of being*".

As an even more telling sign, in the places where we are told that he simply said "*verily, verily, I say to you*", what is actually written on the page is *ahmeyn ahmeyn amar. Amar* does not mean simply "*say*", as in flippantly and casually saying a word, but rather *affirm*. In those cases, he was not flippantly saying "*Assuredly I say to you*" or "*Verily, verily, I say to unto you*", but much more accurately *ahmeyn ahmeyn amar* – "*I am absolutely affirming to you*". Christians need to know this, but unfortunately, many are so locked within the restrictive ideologies of the seemingly safe structures of their religious belief systems that they may never hear the beauty of what the Yeshua teachings were actually seeking to express to us through the ancient Aramaic tongue.

Iman, meaning "*from this fertile, rooted Earth–Center or ground of being*", is much like a linguistic "*ring around a rosy*". We can recall the game so many of us played as a child as we pressed a stick straight into the ground and then danced around that earth-rooted pivot in a joyful circle. We can awaken the ever-enriching depth of our human experience of life by keeping the rooted, fertile earth beneath us central in our awareness as we dance around that still point in our day to day lives.

Experimenting with *Amen* and *Ahmeyn*

Let's try an experiment with toning the word *amen.* Begin with the sound *ay-men*, with the "a" pronounced like the "a" in *base* and the *mehn* sounding just like the word *men.* Tone the *ay-mehn* sound once, while paying close attention to not only the quality of the sound and how it feels, but also to the shape of your face and mouth as you make the sound. How does that feel? As I have said numerous times in this book, there are no right and wrong answers to this experiment. What is of central importance is that we cultivate the experience of openness to experience the sound that we are toning in its purest essence, away from any agreed upon "definitions" of the word. Try it one more time and be aware of the quality of the sound, how you feel as you tone it, as well as the shape and form that your face takes on in its pronunciation: *ayyyye-mehhhhhn.*

Now let's try it beginning with the *ah* sound as in box. Again, be aware of the quality of the sound, how you feel as you tone it, as well as the shape or form that your face takes on as you tone it. *Ahhhhh-mehhhhhn.* How does the *ah* sound and feel in relation with the *aye* sound that we toned before? Try toning the two sounds back and forth a few times: *ahhhhhh* and *ayyyyye.* Again, there is no right or wrong answer to how these sounds feel to us. Just be curious and allow yourself to be open to the experience itself. I ask you to feel out the qualities of the sound with the sole intent of opening you to the feminine experience of being rather than simply the masculine definitions we label the sound with.

Okay, let's try one last experiment with the toning of the word *amen.* This time, pronounce it as the *ah* in "*box*" and the sound of *main*, as in Main Street. Again, be open to how this sound feels within your body: *ahh-main.* How does this feel in relation with all of our previous intonings of this word? Try it again: *ahhhhhh-main.* Though there are several other ways we could pronounce this deeply sacred word, we are going to stop with this one, as it is likely the closest to its ancient pronunciation, though some may debate that. Again, the practice of toning is not about perfect pronunciation or even about the words and sounds themselves. The practice of consciously toning sacred words and sounds is about the experience itself! This is about how we feel as we tone these sounds and how these feelings relate with and influence the state of our consciousness and awareness.

"When joy does come, it should be celebrated, although many of us are embarrassed by spontaneous bursts of elation. It's not that we think there's something wrong with being joyful, but that we have a notion it's not cool or sophisticated to be too joyful, or too openly emotional. We're often as uncomfortable about having hearts as we are about having bodies."

GABRIELLE ROTH
From the book "*Maps to Ecstasy*"
[New World Library]

Chapter 15

Guidance on the Path

This final section of the book is offered as a guiding light for newbies on integrating the process of conscious vocal toning into your daily spiritual practice. When one is wholly open in the process, there are no hard and fast rules, only varying degrees of experiential realization. Knowing what you are doing is of almost no importance. What is important is that you remain curious, observant and open to the experience in this present moment. Experiment by toning in nature, in your car when stuck in traffic, and especially in groups. Most of all, *have fun with the experience!* Here are a few suggestions:

Be open in the experience and allow the sound to birth itself through you

The most vital key in experiencing the depth of vocal toning is that before you utter even one single sound, first be fully present, conscious of your breath, and remain open to the direct experience of these sacred tones and words. The process of vocal toning as a spiritual practice is not in any way about seeking to make perfect, unwavering and flawless sounds. In decades of consciously toning, I have come to very clearly see that when we seek to perfect the sound that is coming out of our mouth, it often begins to waver and wobble.

However, when I let go and allow my deeper awareness to be fully open in the experience of the sounds emerging through me, the sounds take care of themselves. In other words, the more fully I allow myself to let go of how it sounds and instead bring the depth of my awareness back to where I am birthing the sound from in the depth of my being, the result is a more crystalline, open and unwavering tone in direct proportion to my openness to allow the sound to consciously birth *through* me.

Focus on the feminine vowel sounds and allow the masculine consonants to soften

Accentuate the vibratory sound quality of the vowels and allow the consonants to soften and flow as much as possible. As I mention earlier in this book, when toning, focus more on the open, flowing quality of the feminine vowels and allow the more percussive, masculine consonants to soften. Though I do frequently tone with the harder consonant sounds intact, I most often drop the harder consonants and focus on the vowels. Again, there is no rule book here. Be open and allow the process to birth through you.

Experiment with the intensity and pitch of your toning

Try your toning in various keys and intensities: High–Middle–Low; Loud–Soft, *"Under your breath"*, etc. Each has its own unique quality in relation to each term. One thing that I discuss in my toning circles and gatherings is that each person's resonant frequency or "sweet spot" is personal. As I mentioned earlier, the pitch that would resonate for someone with a low voice would obviously be different from the pitch that would inspire a soprano. I will also say that early morning will offer us a lower vocal range as opposed to later in the day when our voices have been toned up and exercised for several hours. It is only by experimenting with pitch, moving the tone up and down in the frequency range, as well as experimenting with the intensity of each tone, that we find the range that "pops" for each one of us.

When you do discover this sweet spot, you may find yourself feeling as if you are being pulled into a vortex-like state of being in which you feel much more as if you are "being toned" rather than simply toning a sound or word. When we do hit this magic realm in toning, our voice seems to take on a life of its own. I often hear various overtones and undertones integrated within the sound that I am toning. The best that I can say is that you will "know it when you hit it". Follow your heart and be open within the process.

Let go and release all inhibitions and self-judgment

Release any inhibitions and self-judgment about how you think you sound, ie: pitch, strength, duration, etc. What is most important is how you *feel.* You may find that the tones often appear to take on a life of their own, and this is when the magic happens!

Focus your toning on specific areas throughout your body

As much as possible, allow yourself to fully feel these vibrations *somatically* – throughout your entire body temple. Also, try bringing your awareness to particular areas of the body temple during your practice, such as your heart, toes, head or to a specific chakra. Be aware of the vibrational echoes that resonate throughout your body *after* the toning.

One of the more deeply profound and feminine experiences for me in my toning practice is being open and curious to the echoing vibrations that continue to resonate and reverberate throughout my body after the actual toning has stopped. In groups, I will often have us focus on a specific tone with increasing intensity for several minutes before counting backward "*three – two – one – stop!*" at which point the entire group stops instantaneously "on a dime".

The result is a sensation that I can imagine it would be like running straight toward a thousand-foot-high cliff at top speed before stopping abruptly right at the edge, with your toes just over the precipice. I utilize this exercise not to "get a buzz" or to get "stoned on God" but rather to cultivate our inherent awareness of the much subtler frequencies of life and vibration through what Yeshua called our *hykla* – our energetic body temple. The more we foster our awareness of these much subtler feminine and experiential forces in our perception, the more our heart is able to open, and, as a result, the deeper the breadth of our awareness of the sacred and divine within the seemingly mundane everyday activities of our daily life.

TONING WITH CHILDREN

Toning with our children can be one of the most blissful, joyous and rewarding experiences as a parent. Even if we have no children of our own, we can offer the bare essentials of our toning practice in the service of our young ones through a streamlined experience minus an excess of commentary and over-definition.

The one thing that I noticed immediately when I began to tone with children is that they do not care all that much about what the word or sound that they are toning means in terms of a descriptive definition in words. They just want to experience and *feel* its direct meaning *within themselves.* I often offer up ancient toning words into a group of adults without first defining those words and then ask them for their perceptions of how the sound *feels* to them. *What does it feel like it means?* There are no right and wrong definitions, much like how numerous cultures can view different meanings of basic root sounds which may or may not relate to the meaning of those sounds or words in another language.

In my experience, this is often the best way to begin with children. Have them tone and then ask them *how it feels.* After hearing a few responses, ask a few more questions. Does it feel open or closed? Do you feel an ease or a strain in the sound? How about your awareness, do you feel more connected, are you more aware of your breathing now? Do not make the mistake of shying away from using words that may seem above the heads of the children. The children coming through today are much more awake and able to quickly grasp the context of spiritual words than many adults may be open enough to realize.

The key here is less in the words that you are using with the children but much more so about you speaking from within a state of conscious presence and not talking too much. Let them speak for themselves. Let them have fun and play with the sounds. Help them cultivate awareness in the words that they are speaking through your own example of this. Our young light beings are much more interested in *how* you are speaking with them than in the meaning of what you think you are saying. The tone or presence – or lack thereof – in our words is of much more importance to a child than what our preconceived definition of those words and phrases will ever be.

For parents, try sitting across from your child, hands together, as you tone. Try it with your eyes open as well as closed. Trade off with one of you toning while the other listens and feels within. Tone together, with eyes open and eyes closed. Stay tuned for much more from me in the future about toning with and for children. They are our future as well as our teachers right now in this present moment. The more we open our hearts with them and express the strength of our own vulnerability, the more we help them cultivate the strength of letting go within themselves.

A Few Tips for Toning with Children

❖ Try to keep your toning session to no more than 30 minutes. If after 30 minutes, they are still asking for more toning, try to cap it at 45 minutes. If this is your first time toning with this group of children, 15 minutes might be even better. Pay attention to the energy in the room and to their attention level.

❖ Start with toning basic, simple sounds like *mmmmmm*, *ahhhhhh* or *ooooooo.*

❖ Let go of the need for them to understand what you think they should be getting about the definition of the word or sound. This experience is not about masculine, specific mental definitions of what the words do or do not mean in any particular language. This is much more about our feminine perception of how the sound *feels* within us. Children will naturally keep you focused on this truth during the toning. They want to *feel* it!

- Talk less and ask more. Toning is not about imprinting our perceived definition of these words and sounds into the mind of the group. This is about allowing them to trust their inner dialogue within the experience itself and to be curious about how these sounds *feel to them.* Ask questions and encourage open dialogue with the children. Keep your mouth shut and listen. You may be surprised with what you learn from them. Let go of any desire to be "the teacher" and just be open.

TONING FOR FAMILIES

Much like toning with children, toning as a family can open up and awaken dimensions within relationships that may have otherwise remained dormant and unrecognized. The earlier a family begins toning, the more natural it will feel as your children grow into young adulthood. If you begin later, with teenagers, you may experience a bit more of a challenge in your attempt to get them to sit still and be fully present.

I hear feedback all the time from families who have found toning to be a very profound method of moving beyond the veils and barriers that can enter into a family as children grow into puberty and beyond. Again, the earlier you begin a regular practice of toning, the smoother the transition will be as your children grow into their teen years and begin to shun any "uncool" aspects of family life. Those who have lived through this experience will know exactly what I am speaking of!

Have your family sit facing each other in a circle, hands entwined. Close your eyes and reintegrate within the present moment. Take three deep cleansing breaths together. Breathe in through your nose, hold it in your lungs for a few moments, and then exhale fully through your mouth. Visualize yourself breathing in the *hayye* or *chi* – the vital life essence – and hold that energy in your body temple for a few moments, and then exhale, releasing all thought, concerns and mental patterns. Just let go. Do this three times together.

One toning sound that teenagers seem to embrace more naturally than some other tones is *ra.* As I mentioned earlier in the book, *ra* is an ancient sound that signified a "*shining or radiating forth of heat and light*". Again, the true spark of a transformational experience with toning, whether individually or in a group, is not so much in holding the meaning of the sound in your mind so much as being open and aware of the direct experience of the present moment. Let go of any and all thought processes; Remain open in your absolute willingness to feel the sound as it manifests itself through you. Remain curious and open.

Tone the *ra* sound seven times together. Find a common ground pitch that is comfortable enough for everyone to have a deep experience and bring yourselves fully into the feeling of the tone. *Ra* is a very powerful, opening tone that, if practiced with full awareness, has a "peeling back the veils" quality to it. It is most pronounced in its power to stimulate and open the third eye and crown chakras. After toning *ra* seven times, you may feel a slight dizziness or disoriented feeling in your head. After the toning, sit in silence together, hands still entwined, and savor the sweet heady wine of the tone's reverberating echoes through your body temples.

Experiment with other simple tones and words while seated in the circle, both with and without your hands joined together. Be aware of the experiential qualities of varying your attention from the sound you are making, to the sound another family member is making, or the sound of everyone as a whole. Be aware of the echoing layers of space all around you in your environment as the tones bounce off of your surroundings. Allow the toning to open your awareness into some of the much subtler, less obvious feminine forces at work in your family relationships. As I so often say, the true "magic" of relationships exists not so much in the obvious, manifest strata of everyday life so much as in the much more intangible, subtly perceived qualities of the heart and deeper layers of awareness. Be open.

TONING FOR COUPLES

Toning can be a great tool in the healthy growth of any relationship, whether it be for couples, friends, family members, co-workers or even pets and plants. For couples, toning can be embraced as a way of nurturing intimacy, authenticity and openness. If practiced wholeheartedly, toning can be an avenue to the opening of the heart and the awakening of selfless vulnerability in close relationships.

Sit across from your partner, face to face and hand in hand. Close your eyes and spend a few moments reintegrating within the present moment. Take three deep cleansing breaths together. Breathe in through your nose, hold it in your lungs for a few moments, and then exhale fully through your mouth. Visualize yourself breathing in the *hayye* or *chi* – the vital life essence – and hold that energy in your body temple for a few moments, and then exhale, releasing all thought, concerns and mental patterns. Just let go. Do this three times together.

Now mindfully open your eyes, seeing deeply into each other's soul. Let go of any need to do or give anything. Just be in the moment. You may notice that your attention keeps jumping from one of their eyes to the other. If this happens, try focusing completely on your partner's left eye or on the space above and between their eyes. Now take three more deep cleansing breaths together, just as you did a few moments earlier, though this time, keep your eyes focused deeply into each other's being.

Start with a very basic sound together, such as *mmmmmmmm*. Tone the sound three times together. The sound *mmmm* is the Aramaic/Hebrew letter *mem*, which means *water* or *vast expanse*. Be aware of the open, flowing quality of the sound. Again, let go of any need to do or "give" anything to your partner, simply be open in the experience of the tone itself while gazing into each other's eyes. Now add the *ah* sound – the letter *alef* – to the *mem*, to create the sound *maaaaaaaaa*. Tone this sound *maaaaaaaaa* three times together.

Now, add the sound *ya* to the end of *ma* to create the sound *maya*. Again, *maya* or *mayim* is the Aramaic word for *water*. The *aya* sound at the end means something that has no boundaries – no beginning and no ending. In Sanskrit, *maya* is the flowing, visionary world of liquid illusion. Rather than focusing in any way on what the sound *means*, just allow yourselves to be open in the direct experience of how the tone *feels* within yourselves and in relationship with your partner.

Experiment by varying your focus between the sound coming out of your own temple to the sound emanating from your partner, as well as to the intermingling of both sounds in relationship within each other. Also be aware of the tones echoing back from the walls, objects, trees or space around you. Fostering our awareness of the multitudes of sound and vibrational layers nested within and around us as one singular, unified aspect of being can be one of the most fruitful and rewarding experiences in the process of vocal toning. This can also be an open door to enriching our relationships to other beings – human, animal, plant or inanimate.

Experiment with different basic sounds and words. Be sure to integrate generous spaces of stillness and silence, remaining keenly aware of the non-verbal reverberations that echo throughout the body temple *after* the tones. Here, in this open, vulnerable, feminine space, lies the open portal to a truly magical relationship. True intimacy lies not in the multitudes of words and actions that we experience together on the apparently physical level, but rather within the much subtler feminine, less defined and intangible senses of the true non-dual being. This is where the divine relationship lives, moves and has its being – within the open spaces of what John Steinbeck called the one "*great big soul*". Let go and she will reveal her essence *through you, AS you* while she sheds the essence of her holy breath upon your sacred relationship.

The Key to Toning is in the Process Itself

The further down the road that I walk with the process of toning and chanting, the more deeply I connect with the truth that *the map is not the terrain.* Talking *about* it can never take the place of actually *doing* it. We must let go of our pursuit for perfect technique and *just do it.* There is literally no right or wrong way to tone. The simple act of just humming or toning a simple tone, sound, word or phrase, has helped me through some of the most intense, challenging experiences of my entire life. It was there for me throughout the dissolution of my parents' marriage, for the birth of my children, and in the death of my mother.

Let go of any thought or judgment of whether you are doing it "right" or if the sound of your voice is good enough. Never mind what its advantages or benefits may be. *Just do it.* You may very well realize a shift in your being that transcends any experience you have ever felt in your entire life. And please do write and let me know how this journey of toning is manifesting for you in your spiritual life. Because of the intensity of my schedule, I will probably not be able to write back, but I will do my best to read it because I care about you deeply. *Yes, YOU.* I am truly and deeply honored to be of service to humanity and service to the Conscious Light of Life Itself.

Ahmeyn.
And so it is.

Dale Allen Hoffman is a "civilian scholar", mystic and healer. Ancient Insight for the Present moment. Rather than studying biblical and religious history from within the fences of theological seminaries and institutions, Dale has chosen to step off the track of religious programming and instead take a path less traveled. Dale encourages others to stop "eating the menu being served" through religious spin-doctoring and manipulation into an authentic, honest investigation of the ACTUAL history of *The Yeshua Teachings* and the Christian philosophy in all of its manifestations.

Dale reveals the much earlier Akkadian, Phoenican, Sumerian and Egyptian frames of mythic symbology and astrotheology which were long ago laid over the stories of and about Jesus. More importantly, Dale shows us why we should not "throw the baby out with the bathwater", but instead allow ourselves to bring the ancient Gnosticism of The Yeshua Teachings into the deepest spaces of our mystical heart, transforming our consciousness right down to the deepest elements of energetic and Tantric alchemy.

Though known worldwide for his decades of study and teachings focused on the Aramaic language attributed to Jesus, Dale's focus is not simply on words or languages alone, but rather on the Gnostic experiential core of how to consciously live the world's great philosophies from the inside out. He burns away the veils of religion, theology, linguistics and mythology with the pure intent of revealing the direct, transformational flame at the heart of The Yeshua Teachings. Dale is not a translator as much as he is an activator – a healing voice for awakening, much like Coleman Barks is for the poetry of *Jalal ad-Din Rumi.*

Dale's work brings forth a direct experience of the profound, transformational qualities of consciously intoned ancient and indigenous sounds, tones and languages on activating states of deep Presence and sound healing. He travels internationally sharing the rich spiritual wisdom which has been veiled beneath almost two millennia of misunderstandings, skewed translations, intentional manipulation and a general lack of spiritual perception. He has published numerous audio and DVD programs. *Echoes of an Ancient Dream* is Dale's first book.

Dale Allen Hoffman lives in Asheville, North Carolina with his beautiful wife Loretta and three indigo children Lucynda, Mikey and Shemaya.

Please visit Dale's website for a series of free videos and mp3 audio downloads produced as accompaniments to this book. Dale shares insights into vocal toning as well as offering guidance for toning the words and sounds contained in Section Three of *Echoes*.

You can also join his email newsletter, view his appearance schedule, purchase CDs, DVDs, books and additional support materials, or schedule events with Dale.

WWW.DALEALLENHOFFMAN.COM

We gratefully accept tithes and donations to help Dale continue spreading the Light to more souls across Mother Earth.

You can write to Dale at:

Dale Allen Hoffman
c/o The Aramaic Healing Circle
PO Box 6447
Asheville, NC 28816 U.S.A.

Made in the USA
Charleston, SC
13 November 2015